P9-CDI-818

THE TRUTH OF THE MATTER

STUDIES IN THE APOSTLES' CREED

By
NORMAN APEL KOOP, M. DIV., Th.M.

© Copyright 1977 by Norman Apel Koop

SERMONS FROM THE APOSTLES' CREED

"I BELIEVE"
Hebrews 11:1

There is only one verse in the Bible which defines faith in a way that no other verse does, and that is Hebrews 11:1. "Now faith is the assurance of things hoped for, the conviction of things not seen." That does not make any sense whatever to the non-Christian. I Corinthians 2:14 says: "But a natural man does not accept the things of the Spirit of God; for they are foolishness to him, and he cannot understand them, because they are spiritually appraised." Faith means to believe. We will come to see also in this study that faith is a gift of God. It is not that which is concocted in the heart or in the mind of man. It is a gift of God given to those of His own choosing. The Scriptures teach that God has given us the faith whereby we are able to believe. (Ephesians 2:8, 9) One of the other introductory precepts that we must understand here is that faith cannot be separated from what you and I call knowledge. Faith and knowledge go hand in hand in the Scriptures. When a man says, "Lord, I believe," he is saying, "Lord, I know You." Paul says in II Timothy 1:12, "For this reason I also suffer these things, but I am not ashamed; for I know whom I have believed and I am convinced that He is able to guard what I have entrusted to Him until that day."

Now faith performs two things. It performs as a substance and it performs as evidence. Thomas Manton differentiated between the performance of faith and the effects of faith. Faith produces primary and secondary blessings in the life of a believer. In Hebrews 11:7 we read the story of Noah's ark coming to rest on Mt. Ararat. "By faith Noah, being warned by God about things not yet seen, in reverence prepared an ark for the salvation of his household, by which he condemned the world, and became an heir of the righteousness which is according to faith." Now faith is a substance of things not seen. It is quite clear from the Genesis account that it had never rained on the earth before in those days. The Garden of Eden was watered by a mist. When the rains came, men were terrified by this new spectacle. It says that the fountains of the deep opened up and the fountains of the heavens poured down. Noah had never understood what that meant, but God said a flood was coming and Noah obeyed in the construction of an ark when he had never yet seen a raindrop! How did Noah do that? By faith! Faith is a link, a conduit which feeds the knowledge of God to us who as natural sinners cannot understand anything spiritual. It is knowledge based upon the mighty acts of God in history. The effects of biblical faith are seen in verses 1 to 11 of Hebrews 11. The performance of faith, however, is found only in the first verse. Now what is faith? I ask the question again. It is the confidence placed in a testimony that you know to be true. You are assured of something, and therefore you act upon it. You know that Mr. Jones is going to meet you in your office tomorrow at ten o'clock and that is why you leave your house at quarter of ten to be there. You cannot see him at the office, but you have the assurance of the knowledge of the character of that man that he is going to be there at ten o'clock and so you endeavor to meet him at that time.

Faith also has to have an object. You cannot just say, "I believe". You will talk to people who think they are Christians and call themselves Christians who say, "Oh, I have faith." Faith in what? Faith in the church? Faith in the minister? That does not count. Faith's object is Jesus Christ's death and resurrection. Those are historical facts which cannot be denied and even though men try to disprove them, the reason that you and I believe them as Christians is not because we have seen them, but because God has given us an assurance and an evidence of things we have not seen. I have not seen the risen Christ but I know Him. Knowledge of God and belief in Him are therefore connected. How can I know that which I have not seen? God has shown it to me. Let me illustrate what it means to act subjectively upon an objective truth. Objective truth is that which God gives to me which I know to be absolutely true and not to be changed. Subjective truth is that which I produce on my own but based upon objective truth which cannot be shaken. You can take cement, sand, lime and water, and produce what you and I call concrete. That is objective truth. You put those things together and mix them to the right proportions and let them dry and you are going to have a concrete block. I know that to be true. But when I take those concrete blocks and build a foundation with them, then I am evidencing my faith in the characteristics of concrete. It is a subjective act upon an objective truth. That God raised Jesus Christ from the dead is objective truth. But when I act upon that which God has done for me and appropriate it for my life, that is subjective exercise of objective truth. It becomes personal.

Now, we need also to talk about the evidence of things not seen. I have spoken about acting subjectively upon an objective truth. We must not forget that faith is never at the mercy of an argument. When you have a nonbeliever standing face to face with a believer, one says, "I believe in God," and the other says, "Prove it," you are at a standoff. But the man who is not a believer in God cannot do anything to upset a man's faith because the man who has faith has a knowledge which is invisible to the nonbeliever. If I believe that stacked up against the wall at the back of this church is an upside-down pink elephant spitting green golf balls from its mouth, there is nothing that you can say to me by scientific proof that will dissuade me of that belief. Can you show me any evidence that will cause me not to believe that there is a pink elephant back there? Faith is never at the mercy of an argument, because faith is given to us by God, and the natural man does not see these things at all. Let me illustrate. A man is standing on a bluff, and he is looking out across a vast plain. There is a man standing on a higher bluff just behind him with a telescope. The first man says, "My, that's a beautiful valley." And the man behind him says, "Yes, but you should see the mountains beyond the valley." And the man on the lower bluff says, "What mountains?" He says, "Can't you see them? Out there are the most glorious peaks I have ever seen." The man on the lower bluff turns around and sees that the man behind him has an instrument which he does not have. That is what it is like when the nonbeliever, the unconverted man, is baffled at the mind of the believer, who says, "I believe in God even though I have never seen the resurrected Christ." What is the telescope he has? What is the vehicle of knowledge that the believer has that the nonbeliever does not have? It is faith! It is the knowledge from God without which he would not even know who He was, let alone what God has done for us.

Now, many say they believe, but the assurance is not there. We say here that we believe that sin is offensive to God, but do we really believe that sin is offensive to God if we keep offending God through cherished sin? We say, "Oh yes, I agree with Jesus when He says that if you gain the whole world and lose your soul, what does it profit you?" But how many of us go about our lives doing anything we possibly can to gain the world and to hell with our souls?

In conclusion, will you look at John 9:24-41. It is the story of a man who had been kicked out of the synogogue because he believed in Jesus. "So a second time they called the man who had been blind, and said to him 'Give glory to God; we know that this man is a sinner.' He therefore answered, 'Whether He is a sinner, I do not know; one thing I do know, that, whereas I was blind, now I see.' They said therefore to him, 'What did He do to you? How did He open your eyes?' He answered them, 'I told you already, and you did not listen; why do you want to hear it again? You do not want to become His disciples too, do you?' And they reviled him, and said, 'You are His disciple; but we are disciples of Moses. We know that God has spoken to Moses; but as for this man, we do not know where He is from.' The man answered and said to them, 'Well, here is an amazing thing, that you do not know where He is from, and yet He opened my eyes. We know that God does not hear sinners; but if any one is God-fearing, and does His will, He hears him. Since the beginning of time it has never been heard that any one opened the eyes of a person born blind. If this man were not from God, He could do nothing.' They answered

8

and said to him, 'You were born entirely in sins, and are you teaching us?' And they put him out.

"Jesus heard that they had put him out; and finding him, He said, 'Do you believe in the Son of Man?' He answered and said, 'And who is He, Lord, that I may believe in Him?' Jesus said to him, 'You have both seen Him, and He is the one who is talking with you.' And he said, 'Lord, I believe.' And he worshiped Him. And Jesus said, 'For judgment I came into this world, that those who do not see may see; and that those who see may become blind.' Those of the Pharisees who were with Him heard these things, and said to Him, 'We are not blind too, are we?' Jesus said to them, 'If you were blind, you would have no sin; but now you say, 'We see;' your sin remains." Note that it was not until the Lord revealed Himself to the man that the man responded in faith by saying, "I believe."

Have you come to that point in your life where you will commit yourself to the One who has revealed Himself to us?

"IN GOD THE FATHER"
John 17:1-3

Let us look at two things here. First, the fatherhood of God and second, the power that has been given to Jesus Christ, as it concerns our salvation by the Father. Someone may ask, "Why do we refer to our God as a Father?" If the man on the street who knew nothing about Christianity or Jesus Christ came to you and said, "Say, I passed by your church the other evening and through the window I heard you reciting some sort of prayer. Who is this Father that you are addressing?", what would you say? Would you be able to say to him, "I am an adopted son and my heavenly Father is God Almighty." In this passage, the Lord Jesus Christ is praying here and that is not to be taken lightly. We do not have many glimpses at conversations between members of the Trinity. We have here, the lengthiest and surely the deepest conversation between any members of the Godhead anywhere recorded in the Scriptures.

God is the Father of our Lord Jesus Christ and Galations 4:6 says this: "And because you are sons, God has sent forth the Spirit of His Son into our hearts, crying 'Abba! Father!' " The word "Abba" means daddy. Paul is telling us we are in a position now as redeemed by Christ to address the Creator of

11

this universe as our "Daddy-Father". If you go to Greece, Turkey, or Lebanon today, the word "Abba" is found freely on the lips of the children. It is not mommy and daddy, but mamma and abba. "Pater" is the formal word for father, but "Abba" is the familiar, intimate friendly term for father.

Now God does not let everyone call Him "Daddy". God does not put Himself into a position where men are able to do that in a willy-nilly fashion. God has only one unique begotten Son, but God has millions of adopted sons. Although the male term is used here in the Scriptures, of course it is understood that daughters is implied under the category of sons. There is a three-fold aspect to God's Fatherhood of Jesus Christ. The first aspect is the incarnation. God the Father was the Father of the physical babe that was born in Bethlehem. We read about this in two places in Scripture. In Hebrews 10:5 we read: "Therefore, when He comes into the world, He says, 'Sacrifice and offering Thou has not desired, but a body Thou has prepared for Me.' " The incarnate Word, Jesus Christ, was prepared by the Father for the particular purpose of bleeding upon a cross on Calvary to purchase certain people from the bondage of sin. Then in Luke 1:35 we read: "And the angel answered and said to her, 'The Holy Spirit will come upon you, and the power of the Most High will overshadow you; and for that reason the holy offspring shall be called the Son of God.' " The Father Almighty, prepared for Himself, a son, physically. That is one of the aspects of the fatherhood of God to Jesus Christ. The second is that Jesus Christ is the first born among many brethren. Those of you who know anything about logic can certainly see the truth here. If we are adopted sons of God the Father Almighty and if Jesus Christ is the unique begotten Son of God the Father Almighty, that makes Jesus Christ and us brethren, and members of the same heavenly family. In Romans 8:29 Paul makes it quite clear: "For whom He foreknew, He also predestined to become conformed to the image of His Son, that He might be the first-born among many brethren." When the Scriptures say that you and I are going to be conformed to the image of Christ, that means that God has prepared a heaven for millions of Jesus Christs. One of them, His unique begotten Son and all the others adopted, but who will inherit the privileges of the Lord Jesus Christ. That is a staggering thought.

But the Scriptures teach us that we will inherit what Jesus Christ has, which makes us brethren.

Interestingly, verse 3 is the only place in the entire Bible where Jesus Christ refers to Himself as Jesus Christ. He calls Himself the Son of man, He calls Himself the door and the Good Shepherd, but this is the only place in the Bible where He refers to Himself as Jesus Christ. Were any to have missed the meaning of the other titles, Christ here tells us that He is Christ and the only way to the Father.

Only you know whether or not you can claim to be a member of God's family. Only you know whether or not you can truly drop to your knees at night and say, "Daddy, I've got some things to talk over with You." You see, if you are not able to approach God in that way, you do not yet know the love of Jesus Christ and what it meant when He bled for you. Are you a member of God's family? How do you know you are a member of God's family? If you were to perish this evening, which is a prospect for any of us, and find yourself standing before the Father Almighty and He says to you, "What right have you to enter into My Kingdom?", what would you answer? The Scriptures say you have only one answer: I come into Your kingdom because You have given me the righteousness of Jesus Christ. I believed in Him.

"ALMIGHTY"
Genesis 17:1

The Biblical doctrine of the sovereignty of God is not taught much today. It was known, as were the Ten Commandments and a lot of other passages that are generally forgotten and ignored, 200 years ago. It has since slipped through the fingers of American Protestantism, so today I believe that the doctrines which are encompassed in the teaching of the sovereignty of God are not only ignored, but are basically disbelieved by most Christians.

What is a sovereign? Historically, a sovereign was a gold coin, minted by the United Kingdom. It had the stamp of the King of England on it and wherever that coin was found in the world it represented the power of the King of England and the power of the Navy of that great Empire. So, the sovereignty of God is the supreme unchallenged authority of God in all things, particularly in the salvation of men. We read in Genesis 17:1 the following: "Now when Abram was ninety-nine years old, the Lord appeared to Abram and said to him, 'I am God Almighty; walk before Me, and be blameless.' "

Let us examine three areas of thought. First, what is the biblical revelation of God's sovereignty as against modern thinking? Second, let us look at God's election and His reprobation of the human race. Third, let us view a little bit about the human will and God's sovereignty.

Fortunately for us, God has told us in His Word who He is and what He is. He is Almighty, He is all wise, He is everywhere at the same time and He is the God that has been revealed to us as One whom we can trust. However, today's understanding in christendom of God's sovereignty is not that at all. Most think God is a frustrated old man who somehow has lost touch with our needs. Arthur W. Pink said, "The God of the popular mind is the creation of a maudlin sentimentality." The Church today also implies that God's plan of salvation, which is elective, redemptive and applied, is at best hopeful, and at worst defeated. Most Christians, and certainly non-Christians just do not talk today about the many passages in Scripture which teach us that God has planned all of salvation from the beginning to the end and that He brings us to understand these things in our own lifetime. Who, today, is teaching that God chooses particular people unto salvation? Where do you hear today it being taught that Jesus Christ died for a specific host of people? Where do you hear it taught today that the Holy Spirit applies the knowledge of those things to our hearts, that we do not somehow dream them up or earn them? Those are foreign concepts to the ears of most men. Why is that so? Because we live in an age where man is supposed to have all the answers, and God is growing old. Yet, that is not the God that I know. That is not the God of Holy Scripture. The God of the untaught Christian is like a man who is bowling. He throws the ball down the alley and he hops up and down on one foot having absolutely no idea what pins will be struck, and if they are struck, whether they will fall down or not. And possibly, the ball will miss them completely and go down the gutter. That is modern man's view of God's control of history. But the Bible teaches us that this bowler controls the ball. The pins are going to go down exactly the way He wants them to fall.

When we speak of the sovereignty of God, we also must mean that God is irresistible. There are many quarters in American Protestantism today that would argue that. They would say, "What? God is irresistible? Of course I can resist God. I don't have to pay any attention to Him." I am sure that is what Abram said, in effect, living with his pagan father, Terah, all those years. Who is God? Who needs Him? Yet, what is it that brought a change in Abram's life all of a sudden? He was brought up in a pagan family and was uneducated. Why is it that all of a sudden he responded to God? Either he was crazy or he fell under the conviction of the Holy God that we know through the Lord Jesus Christ. Abram had not the ability to resist God. Noah had not the ability to resist God. Moses had no ability to resist God and neither do you, if you are in God's plan of salvation. We read in Scripture of the image of the potter and the clay. Today, man says that the lump of clay, given enough time, will form itself into a pot! It is an analogy of how most Christians think they become new creatures in Christ. The theology of God that is propounded today sees the clay molding the pot rather than the other way around. Because that was also the thinking of Paul's day, he discussed it in Romans 9. In looking at Romans 9 you will find some of the most devastating answers in the entire Scriptures to man's arguments that God is not fair in the way He conducts His business. We can say of a human being that what he does is not fair, and we might be able to justify it. It is not so with God because His perfect standards are seen by imperfect man to be outside his realm of practice. In Romans 9:14-20 we read: "What shall we say then: There is no injustice with God, is there? May it never be! For He says to Moses, 'I will have mercy on whom I have mercy, and I will have compassion on whom I have compassion.' So then it does not depend on the man who wills or the man who runs, but on God who has mercy. For the Scripture says to Pharaoh, 'For this very purpose I raised you up, to demonstrate My power in you, and that My name might be proclaimed throughout the whole earth.' So then He has mercy on whom He desires, and He hardens whom He desires.

You will say to me then, 'Why does He still find fault? For who resists His will?' On the contrary, who are you, O man, who answers back to God? The thing molded will not say to the molder, 'Why did you make me like this?'' God is not accountable to His creatures for what He does. But you will not find that to be popular thinking among people who call themselves Christians. They will say, "God owes me an explanation." But He does not.

God also is sovereign in mercy. Look at John 5:3-9. This is an expansion upon the Romans 9 passage. In John 5:3-9 we see that God is sovereign and all powerful in mercy. Is God merciful to all men? No, not regarding salvation. He extends common grace as seen in Matthew 5:43-48, but He is not merciful to all men regarding salvation. Look at John 5:3-9: "In these lay a multitude of those who were sick, blind, lame, withered. And a certain man was there, who had been thirty-eight years in his sickness. When Jesus saw him lying there, and knew that he had already been a long time in that condition, He said to him, 'Do you wish to get well?' The sick man answered Him, 'Sir, I have no man to put me into the pool when the water is stirred up, but while I am coming, another steps down before me.' Jesus said to him, 'Arise, take up your pallet, and walk.' And immediately the man became well, and took up his pallet and began to walk. Now it was the Sabbath on that day." Of all of those sick, lame and crippled people that were sitting around the pool of Bethesda, only one of them is singled out for mercy. But you say to me, "God is merciful to all men." Well, then, why does Jesus pass up the others? God is merciful to whom He will be merciful and we cannot say to God, "That is not fair." Consider also God's response to Moses in Exodus 4:10, 11. "Then Moses said to the Lord, 'Please Lord, I have never been eloquent, neither recently nor in time past, nor since Thou hast spoken to Thy servant; for I am slow of speech and slow of tongue.' And the Lord said to him, 'Who has made man's mouth? Or who makes him dumb or deaf, or seeing or blind? Is it not I, the Lord?'" These so-called mistakes of nature are the manifestations of a sovereign God who wills certain of His creatures to be born blind or perfect, deaf or whole, dumb or vocal. We do not need to go any farther than the story in the Gospel of John where a man was born lame for one purpose: that in his healing, Jesus would be glorified. When you understand that God will do things like that to glorify His own name, you are understanding that God is sovereign and that He does not need us. It does not matter to Him whether we are blind, or crippled, or lame. What matters to Him is that He is glorified in us.

The clearest verse in the entire Scripture about God's elective grace is Ephesians 1:4, where from "before the foundation of the world" God chose unto salvation those who would be His. But do not stop there. Read on. What does it say? Why did He do that? "That we should be holy and blameless before Him." God has redeemed you because He wants you to reflect His character in what you do and in what you say.

God is also sovereign in the gift of His love. Look at John 3:27. "John answered and said, 'A man can receive nothing, unless it has been given him from heaven.' " How do we become saved? By something that we do? Or is it given to us from a God who gives us all things by His grace? Why did God chose Israel out of all the nations of the earth? Why did God choose Isaac over Ishmael? Why did God choose Jacob over Esau? Who are you, O man, to say to the potter, why have you made me thus? God is a sovereign God. He can do what He wants, when He wants and He is not accountable to us for doing those things.

Furthermore, what of election and reprobation? Extract sovereignty from God and you also extract the godhood from God. Let me make this more clear from the Scriptures as it is the true teacher. The fact that God has ordained some to eternal life, which is our focus of attention here at this point, is found in Romans 3:8, "And why not say (as we are slanderously reported and as some affirm that we say), 'Let us do evil that good may come?' Their condemnation is just." What Paul is saying there is that the Christian cannot take the attitude: "now that I am chosen of God, I can do evil." That man's condemnation is just. I do not know any individual who is a believer in Christ who has this attitude. Now I want to emphasize that my preoccupation at this point is not with reprobation. That happens simply by God's passing over the rest of the human race. What I am dealing with at this point is God's elective grace, that He is a God who chooses whom He wants to choose. If you are having difficulty understanding that, I believe that the true appreciation of the doctrine comes only when every member of the family of God realizes that he deserves hell, not heaven. Show me a man who says that he does not deserve hell and I will show you a man who has not yet grasped what salvation means. If you think that somehow you were a "neutral" and that God took you out of that state you do not understand salvation. The Spirit convicts us that our sin will require our lives, and it is out of that pit that God has chosen us and Jesus Christ has redeemed us. I deserve to be in hell. I have absolutely no right to be in heaven. The only way I am getting into heaven is by Jesus Christ's blood shed for me. I cannot work my way in, I am not as strong as God, I cannot convince Him by an argument, I only can claim that which He has already given to me.

I have pointed out Ephesians 1:4. The opposing verse is in Matthew 7:23. I want to underscore one particular word in the verse. In Matthew 7:22, 23 we read: "Many will say to Me on that day, 'Lord, Lord, did we not prophesy in Your name, and in Your name cast out demons, and in Your name perform many miracles?' And I will declare to them, 'I never knew you; depart from Me, you who practice lawlessness.' " Now if Jesus is going to be able to say to many people, "I never knew you," that means that it was never even in His contemplation to save those individuals. They were not in His plan to be saved. By now I trust that you will agree with me that this is not a popular teaching. Nevertheless, the Scriptures teach it and we must teach it.

Finally, let us take a look at the classical argument of the freedom of the will versus God's sovereign will. We have seen that He is sovereign and that He is all powerful. Take away His sovereignty and you take away the God of the Scriptures. We have seen that He is an elective God, and that by passing over others God knew and had foreordained most of the human race to be damned. Where does the human will fit in? Men will say, "Oh, but the Scriptures say, 'Whosoever will'." But of course, those who quote that verse take it out of context and do not read what follows. The key verse here is Philippians 2:13. "For it is God who is at work in you, both to will and to work for His good pleasure." So, is it the man involved who wills to do God's will, and who does it? Or is it God in us who wills to do what God wants us to do? It is clearly the latter, and it is illustrated by the movement of the hand in a puppet. It is unpopular to say that a man's will is dead and that it has nothing to do with his salvation; and unpopular we shall remain, because the world's hatred of God will always remain; the world's persecution of the Church will always remain; but God's Word will always remain. Give the glory to God. He is the One who is responsible for our salvation. Romans 3:11 says that there is none that seek after God. God is not a liar, is He? Does He really mean that? Do you mean that there is not one man across the path of human history that has ever sought God? Yes, no man has ever sought God. (Romans 3:11) But has God sought us? He has not only sought us out, but He has died for us and He has sent the Spirit into our hearts crying, "Abba, Father". Now that is a Gospel which no man can change and which no man can turn around. Yet, someone comes to you and says, "Oh, but the Bible says, 'Whosoever will'." Yes, it does, but read on. Look at John 6:35-37: "Jesus said to them, 'I am the bread of life; he who comes to Me shall not hunger, and he who believes in Me shall never thirst. But I said to you, that you have seen Me, and yet do not believe. All that the Father gives Me shall come to Me; and the one who comes to Me I will certainly not cast out.' " Why is that last part of the verse so often quoted out of context? People quote, "Whoever comes to Me I will in no wise cast out." True! But who are those that come? The first part of the verse tells us that the ones who come to Christ are the ones that God has given to Christ which means that they must be God's possession already. A man chooses that which is according to his nature. Can you remember the time that you did not know Christ and did not want to know Him? What took place between that time and now? God supernaturally intervened in your life which deserved no intervention.

Does it lie within a man's power to yield to God? No! Can that which is filthy clean itself? John 6:44 says: "No one can come to Me, unless the Father who sent Me draws him; and I will raise him up on the last day."

"MAKER OF HEAVEN AND EARTH"
Psalm 19, Genesis 1

I want to examine God's natural creation and God's supernatural creation. We read in Psalm 19:1-6 very powerful words about what the created order, particularly that of the heavens, has to do with teaching us that there is a God, and what Genesis 1:1-5 teaches us. We read in Psalm 19:1-6, "The heavens are telling of the glory of God; and their expanse is declaring the work of His hands. Day to day pours forth speech, and night to night reveals knowledge. There is no speech, nor are there words; their voice is not heard. Their line (sound) has gone out through all the earth, and their utterances to the end of the world. In them He has placed a tent for the sun, which is as a bridegroom coming out of his chamber; it rejoices as a strong man to run his course. Its rising is from one end of the heavens, and its circuit to the other end of them; and there is nothing hidden from its heat." Now, in those particular verses there is a very clear revelation of what the heavens tell us about God and about His glory.

I believe that man was created erect for a purpose. We do not crawl about on our bellies, nor do we move around on our hands and knees. Man, of all creatures who have been made erect, has intelligence far outreaching anything else in the

23

animal kingdom, and still he denies the very God whose heaven is constantly in his vision. These verses in Psalm 19 tell us that the heavens declare the glory of God. What that means is that there is no moment at which the heavens are not speaking of God's glory. The heavens declare not merely a glory created by God but the glory of God in particular. It is not just there to look at and say, "Isn't that pretty?" A man who can really scan the universe and come to the conclusion that he is an atheist, must also come to the conclusion that he is an idiot, on a rational basis alone. Yet, even if God chose to rearrange the constellations so that they spelled out "Jehovah is God", men would still look at that and say, "I do not believe it." There is a story of a little boy who was so successful in flying his kite on a windy day that it went out of sight. It was so far up in the clouds and the mist that he lost the sight of it and someone came along and said, "What are you doing?" He said, "I'm flying a kite, can't you see?" The person said, "No, I can't see. How do you know there is a kite out there?" The boy said, "Because I can feel the tugging of the string." That is an illustration of the natural man's attitude toward the Christian who says, "I know the God of the universe." The Christian knows He is there because of his particular relationship with Jesus Christ.

Now I want to turn to Genesis 1. When I speak of God's supernatural creation, I am speaking of His regenerative work in our hearts. I am not talking about my flesh and my blood and my bones. I am talking about the work that God did in me by taking me as a sinner that was perishing to hell and regenerating me by His Holy Spirit as having been purchased by Christ's blood. The Scriptures teach us that we are new creatures in Christ. I am a brand new creation that did not exist before Christ entered me. Look at Genesis 1:1-5 "In the beginning God created the heavens and the earth. And the earth was formless and void, and darkness was over the surface of the deep; and the Spirit of God was moving over the surface of the waters. Then God said, 'Let there be light'; and there was light. And God saw that the light was good; and God separated the light from the darkness. And God called the light day, and the darkness He called night. And there was evening and there was morning, one day." In those five verses we have a very clear picture of the way God saves men if we understand the relationship between light and darkness as it is described here. I do not wish to force upon this text something that is not there. But I do believe heartily, as Thomas Watson has said, "Only a diamond can cut a diamond; only Scripture can comment effectively upon Scripture." Whether we see it or not, I believe that there is a connection between Genesis 1 and Psalm 19. Every man who is saved, is saved by God's grace. That means that he is not saved by anything to be found in him. Look at the second verse here: "The earth was formless and void." Does that not describe the condition of the human heart before God's light comes into it? The person who is a sinner without the knowledge of Christ is formless. He is empty and he has nothing by which he can claim any value or any worth. This is the state of the human heart before God comes into it. Now we understand from verse 3 onward that life enters the creation narrative. We will all agree, I trust, that life is sustained by light. If our life is dependent upon light, and the created order was dependent upon light, I believe there is a connection between the natural creation and the supernatural creation. The connecting link is simply this: no man knows God until God's light has pierced his soul. Man never comes to the decision that he is worthless in God's sight until he first understands that he is lost.

When you look upon the cross of Christ, we are to see the enactment of a plan that was in God's mind from eternity whereby Jesus Christ was to die for God's people. When that ransom was secured, all of God's people were secured. Some of them come to know that as children, some of them come to know that in their twenties, others may go to eighty years of age before the Holy Spirit applies the knowledge of that redemption to them. Nevertheless, we must agree that we cannot see our sin or our need for Christ until God's light exposes it to us. Dr. Barnhouse told a story to illustrate this truth. A man who was on his way to a party was walking down the city streets after a long afternoon rainstorm. A taxicab carelessly came by very close to the curb, hit a muddy puddle, and splashed him with water. He looked down upon himself in the dark street and didn't see much that should make him go home and change his clothes, so he said to himself, "I'll keep going." But as he approached a streetlamp on the corner, the more he saw that he was not acceptable in the way he stood to go to that particular engagement. This is exactly what God does to us in the beginning of making us aware of our salvation. We are stained deeply with sin, we are born with it, it is indelibly inscribed upon our nature and without the light of Christ, we look at ourselves and we say, "I'm not so bad. I'll keep walking my own way." Then all of a sudden the piercing light of God's sovereign grace comes into our lives and we see our nature in the light of Jesus Christ. We then see we are not acceptable to God as we are. What is the remedy? We are given the robe of righteousness of Christ. The Spirit of God applies the redemption of Christ's blood to us. He regenerates our spirits and we are on the way to repentance and the long glorious pilgrimage of the Christian life. So, just as light was an early work in the creation narrative of Genesis 1, light is also an early work in our salvation. I believe that God takes His time in certain people to plant the seeds, but that the light comes instantaneously when it comes.

There is another interesting parallel here which is so obvious that we overlook it. Darkness was there until the light came. That means that God's light is irresistible. As long as these lights are on in this building, there can be no darkness to resist it. It is only when the light is withdrawn or if it is absent that darkness is present. That is exactly the way it is with the human heart. It is dark, but once the light enters it, it cannot resist the light. That is a glorious message! Nothing in the sinner's life can quench that light. Now look at verse 4. We have seen the darkness of the human heart, we have seen that light is necessary to expose it, we have seen that the darkness cannot resist the light. Now in verse 4 we read: "And God saw that the light was good; and God separated the light from the darkness." Philippians tells us that we are persuaded that He who has begun a good work in us will complete it unto the day of Jesus Christ. (Philippians 1:6) That means that when God's light comes into your heart, He is just beginning His work in you. It is never withdrawn. Never! It says here that God divided the light from the darkness. Does this not speak of the civil warfare that takes place in the Christian's life? You say, "What do you mean, a civil war?" I mean that the dark nature that I once served, wars against the new creation of Christ Jesus. The

26

darkness cannot resist the light, it cannot overcome the light, but that hunger to let it revive still remains in the Christian heart. Well, if God has divided the light and the darkness, and Christians also learn early in their life what it means to be warring against the flesh, then we also can understand how God names the light and the darkness and what they have to do with our understanding of the order of our spiritual progress. Verse 5 says: "And God called the light day, and the darkness He called night. And there was evening and there was morning, one day." You see, if I had written that verse, I would have said, "And God called the light day, (that comes first) and the darkness night, (that comes second)." Why does God put the evening first? Because that was what *was* first. Darkness. Formlessness. It was out of the darkness that the light has come, not the other way around.

Now in conclusion, then, if we are naturally children of darkness, and God has given us a new name, (it says here "He called the light day",) we who are naturally children of wrath have been called the children of light. We have inherited that which is Jesus Christ's. His light is in us. We have been separated from the powers of darkness and we are in His hands. God makes all things new and He does it all alone. Do not be like the drunkard who came home late one night and saw that his wife had left a candle flickering in the window for him. But because he was so drunk, he saw two candles, and he said to himself, "I'll just blow out one of them and I will be able to get through the house by the light of the other." When he blew out the light, all the light was gone and there he stood in the darkness. That is just like the man who plays with God's Gospel. Do not think you can play with God. I do not want you to procrastinate.

There is a story of a ship at the turn of the century by the name of the Central American and it started to sink. The captain of the sinking ship put out a distress signal and another ship came near. The captain of the rescuing ship asked, "What's wrong?" The first captain said, "We're taking in water, but we are going down very slowly, will you lie by until morning and take on our passengers?" The captain of the other ship said, "Lie by I will, but let me take your passengers now." The captain kept saying, "Lie by till morning and take the

passengers then; lie by till morning, take the passengers then."
When morning came there was no ship and there were no
passengers. I invite you to come to Christ even though it is God
who must bring you to Christ. In the last chapter we saw that
God has taken His elect and has given them to Christ. Well, if
God has already given you to Christ, what are you waiting for?
Come! If you are in God's family, you will come. Why not
accept Him now? Do not be the drunkard who wants to blow
out only one candle, because they will both go out.

"AND IN JESUS CHRIST HIS ONLY SON, OUR LORD"
John 10:11

Jesus Christ is OUR Lord. In other words He is the Lord of Christians only. John 10:11 says, "I am the good shepherd; the good shepherd lays down His life for the sheep." Now it is commonly misunderstood that Jesus Christ died for the sins of the entire world. He did not. This is the doctrine of particular redemption. There are three divisions to our outline. The first shows Jesus Christ the good shepherd contrasted to the hireling. Secondly, Jesus Christ died for the sheep, and we need to know who the sheep are. And thirdly, what was the extent of the atonement of Jesus Christ?

We are not talking about the nature of the atonement but how far reaching it is, i.e., to whom is it applied.

The first part of John chapter 10 contrasts the good shepherd with the hireling. It simply makes the distinction that the shepherd looks after the welfare of the sheep because he loves the sheep. The hireling looks after the welfare of the sheep only because he is getting paid for doing so. The Lord Jesus Christ does not treat the sheep that way. He has died for the sheep and the Lord Jesus Christ has fulfilled His work by contract with the Father. When He died upon the cross that was for a specific host of people.

Secondly, Jesus Christ lays down His life for the sheep. It should be noted that the shepherd lays down His life for the sheep voluntarily. Jesus Christ died because He wanted to. He was ordained from eternity to die according to the Father's Will, but no one can say that Jesus Christ went to the cross against His own Will. He wanted to do it because He loved us and knew for whom He was dying. This is one of the many passages where we also get a clear focus on just why Jesus Christ died. There are many confused notions as to why Christ died. Some people believe that Jesus Christ died as a martyr for some cause, which was not quite clear. Others believe that Jesus Christ died to set an example for suffering, which is sheer nonsense. Jesus Christ died, fulfilling the Will of the Father, for a specific host of people. He died for them that they might live. In the Old Testament, God declared that it was for the sheep that Jesus Christ was to die. It is in the prophetic 53rd chapter of Isaiah where in verse 8 this is made clear. "By oppression and judgment He was taken away; and as for His generation, who considered that He was cut off out of the land of the living, for the transgression of my people to whom the stroke was due?" Those verses tell us that there was a particular people who deserved the stroke of condemnation but in whose stead Jesus Christ was to come and to pay the debt that they owed to God. In Matthew 1:21, the angel comes to Mary and says to her, "You shall call His name Jesus, for it is He who will save *His* people from their sins."

Furthermore, in Matthew 26:28, it is made even more clear and goes in Titus 2:14. But look at Matthew 26:28, "For this is My blood of the covenant, which is to be shed on behalf of *many* for forgiveness of sins." If you look at Titus 2:14 you will read this: "Who (Jesus Christ) gave Himself for us, that He might redeem *us* from every lawless deed and purify for Himself a people for His own possession, zealous for good deeds." I have said something very briefly about the fact that the good shepherd who lays down his life for the sheep is not a hireling. He is not there to do something because he has to, he does it because He loves us.

Furthermore, we see that Jesus Christ lays down His life for the sheep in verse 11. Let us look at the extent of the atonement which really should consume our time this evening as a focal point upon this text. To say that Jesus Christ died for the sins of the entire world is opening yourself up to a very great mistake, because if Christ died for all men, then all men must be in heaven. You say, "No, some will be in hell." Well, then I ask you, if Christ died for all men and some will be in hell, who will be in heaven? You say to me, "Those who believe." And I ask you, "Who are they that believe?" And whether you know the answer or not, the Scriptures teach us that they who believe are those that the Holy Spirit has given the gift of faith by which they no longer are the natural man who cannot discern the things of the Spirit. They can, now, discern the things of the Spirit by the indwelling of the Spirit of God. The conclusion you must draw, if you believe that Christ died for the sins of the entire world is this: that He died as a collossal mistake and actually saved nobody! The Scriptures teacher that "none seek after God", (Romans 3:11) and if Christ's blood were shed as a blank check for any who *might* come if they wanted to, then we know from the outset that He would have died for nobody, because nobody wants to come to God. Now if there is nobody who seeks God, that means that those who Christ died for were foreknown before the foundation of the world to seek God and if there is a specific host of people whom God foreknew to seek Him, obviously He would have to prompt them to seek Christ because He says in His Word, "No man seeks after God."

We have seen in earlier chapters that God the Father gave a particular people to the Son. Now, what was the Son supposed to do to those people? Hand them back to the Father? His contract with the Father was to die for those whom the Father had given Him to save. There are two passages in the Gospel of John which I believe will make this clear. At least it will remove some of the mud from the waters. The first is in John 6:39, 40. "And this is the will of Him who sent Me, that of all that He has given Me I lose nothing, but raise it up on the last day. For this is the will of My Father, that every one who beholds the Son, and believes in Him, may have eternal life; and I Myself will raise him up on the last day." The unavoidable conclusion is that those whom the Father has chosen were given to the Son that He might not lose any of them but raise them up at the last day. Now look at John 17:9. "I ask on their behalf; I do not ask on behalf of the world, but of those whom Thou has given Me; for they are thine; and all things that are Mine are Thine." God spends almost 15 verses in John 17 to drive home that they who are God's by election are Christ's by redemption. Now that is eternal security! Those that the Father has given to the Son will not be lost.

You see, if Jesus Christ really died in the place of all men, then all men must be saved. Permit me to explain that according to what the Scriptures teach about justification. Let us take ourselves into the legal courtrooms of God. Here is the entire host of the human race that stands guilty and condemned before a holy and righteous God. All of us deserve to be condemned, but the Scriptures teach us that the judgment did not fall upon us, but fell upon Christ. He is the One who had to stand in the dock and was pronounced guilty officially instead of us. And if the Scripture teaches that Jesus Christ was made a curse for His people, then that means we, who are God's people, are set free. But if Christ stood in the dock representing all of humanity, and the judgment of the cross fell upon Him for all men, then all men are set free, not just some. If Jesus really shed His blood for all men, how can any be lost? How could there by any in hell for whom Jesus died? It is tempting to let your emotions run wild here because of your compassion for lost souls. The only reason that you think along those lines is because you love the Lord Jesus and you know what it was like to be without Him. And we do love lost souls and we are to pray for them that we might be instrumental in the calling of them to faith. But let us not permit our emotions to lead us into a direction where we dishonor God's Word. I do not want to stand before the throne of God and say, "Father, there were parts of Your Word which I didn't like, so I didn't talk about them." We are to teach all of Scripture, and we are commanded to know it all.

Again, if Jesus Christ has died for all men, and some are in hell, what security do I have? Here I stand as a professed Christian. I believe that I am saved, but if Jesus died for all men and some of them still slip into hell, what security do I have? I do not have any! I might slip into hell also, because I can say that He died for those who are in hell and He died for me too. Arthur Pink said, "An atonement that fails to atone, and a sacrifice that fails to be a sacrifice is worthless." That is true, is it not? Could Jesus have died for someone who burns in hell? It would not have been a very effective sacrifice. To hold that a man's salvation is dependent upon the sinner's acceptance of Christ on his own is absolutely ridiculous. It is like asking a blind man to read in order to be saved. It is like telling a cripple that he could be saved if he will just get up and walk across the room. How can God, who says that the natural man does not understand salvation, and how can God, who says that "none seek after God", possibly leave it into our hands to accept Him? The entire world would have passed Christ by.

In Romans 8:32 we read: "He who did not spare His own Son, but delivered Him up for us all, all, how will He not also with Him freely give us all things?" Again, if Jesus Christ has died for all men, then all men must receive all things. Is that not what the verse says? But all men do not receive all things. All men certainly do not receive all of the blessings of the Spirit. Now who is wrong? Is God lying or are men's conceptions of the Scriptures perverted? Of course it is the latter. Is it possible to pay a ransom for a prisoner and not have the prisoner free? No. So then, what was the Father's design for Jesus Christ? Did Jesus Christ die to make it possible for a whole race to be saved or did Jesus Christ die to secure permanent salvation for a specific people. I believe the Scriptures teach the latter and teach it most evidently clearly.

The sheep that Christ died for then are God's chosen host. These are the sheep that we read in Ephesians 5:25 in that great marriage passage that Jesus Christ loved the Church and gave Himself up for her. It is the Church, the believers, that Jesus Christ came here to secure. Let us compare two passages of Scripture. They are Matthew 7:23 and II Timothy 2:19. Matthew 7:23 reads: "And then I will declare to them, 'I never knew you; depart from Me, you who practice lawlessness.' " Now look at II Timothy 2:19: "Nevertheless, the firm foundation of God stands, having this seal, 'The Lord knows those who are His,' and, 'Let every one who names the name of the Lord abstain from wickedness.' " Now if the Lord knows those who are His, and He says to some, "I never knew you," then it is quite impossible that God knew or loved all men to the point of salvation. If God can say to one man, "I never knew you, I never considered you unto salvation," then we cannot say that Jesus Christ's atonement was extensive to all men, but only to believers.

Now in conclusion, the opponents to this particular biblical teaching will cite verses like John 3:16 and others and say, "But oh, John 3:16 says, "For God so loved the world, that He gave His only begotten Son, that whoever believes should not perish.'" The last part of that verse I have no problem with at all. 'Whoever believes shall not perish.'" But look just for a moment at what history has told us about the mistake of interpreting a verse like John 3:16 universally. Has God loved the whole world? Well, Romans 1:28 says that He has given the whole world over to a reprobate mind. We went through almost a thousand years of papal darkness, where Bibles were refused to the man and the woman in the pew. How strange of God to say He loves all men throughout all history, when history shows quite clearly that He has not. When we talk about the *world* in a verse like John 3:16, we are talking about it in the sense that God's elect do come from the four corners of the earth. You will see Ugandans, South Americans, Soviet people, Chinese people, Japanese people and Australians in heaven because it has been in God's wisdom to choose some from every nation. (Revelation 5:9) So, when we say God's Son's atonement is efficacious to the sins of the *world*, we have to understand that God's salvation is universal in the sense of Revelation 5:9 only. Salvation cannot mean universal salvation in the sense that all men will be in heaven and hell will be empty. We sing a hymn, "The Church's One Foundation". There is a verse in it that says, "Elect from every nation, yet one o'er all the earth."

Finally, look at John 10:19-31. "There arose a division again among the Jews because of these words." And there has arisen a division in the Church of Christ, nominally speaking, because of these words. "And many of them are saying, 'He has a demon, and is insane; why do you listen to Him?'," Others were saying, 'These are not the sayings of one demon-possessed. A demon cannot open the eyes of the blind, can he?' At that time the Feast of the Dedication took place at Jerusalem; it was winter, and Jesus was walking in the temple in the portico of Solomon. The Jews therefore gathered around Him, and were saying to Him, 'How long will You keep us in suspense? If You are the Christ, tell us plainly.' " If I may indulge in a bit of editorial license here, Jesus asks, "You want it plainly? I will tell it to you plainly. I told you and you did not believe and the works that I do in My Father's name, these bear witness of Me, but you do not believe because you are not of My sheep." The reason they did not believe is because they were not God's people! The good shepherd comes to lay down His life for the sheep and the reason the Pharisees did not understand that is because they were not of the sheep. "My sheep hear My voice, and I know them, and they follow Me; and I give eternal life to them, and they shall never perish; and no one shall snatch them out of My hand. My Father, who has given them to Me, is greater than all; and no one is able to snatch them out of the Father's hand. I and the Father are one.' The Jews took up stones again to stone Him." (Verses 28–31) Men do not like to hear those words. I do not know if you are of the elect of God. I do not know if Christ has actually died for you, but I do know this; that if you come, it is because the Father has given you into the hands of the Savior. Why wait; Eternal security is a security that is redeemed by Christ for the sheep. Christ has died for the believers. Do not fault God because some do not believe. Praise Him because you do. Are you His?

"WHO WAS CONCEIVED BY THE HOLY GHOST, BORN OF THE VIRGIN MARY"
Matthew 1:20

The virgin birth of Jesus Christ is little talked about today and it is decreasingly believed. It is representative of the doctrinal disarray which is being pronounced in the Church. Our purpose in studying the Virgin Birth is not so that we might hold on to some quaint tradition which somehow gets lost underneath the Christmas tree with the tinsel and all the rest of the commercial elements of Christmas, but that we might come to see that without the virgin birth of Jesus Christ, none of us can have any access to God. None of us shall see God if we deny the virgin birth. Now do not get me wrong. Many people are simply ignorant of the virgin birth of Christ and do not know what it means. I am talking about an individual who is cognizant of what the doctrine means and denies it on the basis of what it teaches. That is so serious that they obviously will also have to deny themselves salvation.

Let us look first at the genealogy of Jesus Christ. Our text is Matthew 1:20. "But when he had considered this, behold, an angel of the Lord appeared to him in a dream, saying, 'Joseph, son of David, do not be afraid to take Mary as your wife; for that which has been conceived in her is of the Holy Spirit.' "

But someone will say, "But I thought that God had confined Himself to work within the scope of His own natural laws." Well, in a sense that is true. But God, humanly speaking, goes outside of the bounds of natural laws from time to time and He has in history. The sun stopped for Joshua; in other words, the earth stopped rotating on its axis. Jonah's body after being swallowed by a great fish for three days and three nights, was not decomposed in the acids of that fish's stomach as it certainly normally would have been, but was tossed up upon the shore in normal fashion. And he proceeded on to Ninevah to preach a great revival in that city. We also have it in the resurrection of the Lord Jesus Christ. Those who attack the doctrine of the virgin birth do it on a very shoddy basis. They say, "Oh, it's only mentioned in two gospel accounts, in Matthew and Luke. Mark and John do not even talk about it, therefore it must be a spurious and false doctrine." You can see the foolishness of that kind of teaching because there are other parts of Scripture that those same individuals would not cast out which are certainly only found in *one* place in Scripture.

The following is a lengthy quotation from Dr. Donald Grey Barnhouse in his commentary on Romans. Having never read anything so insightful in this area, I share it with you.

"One of the greatest proofs of the Virgin Birth is in the fact that there are two genealogies of Jesus, one each in Matthew and Luke. It may interest you to know how I once set forth this proof before a class in university. When I returned to America in 1925 after seven years of travel and study in Europe, I became an assistant in the history department of the University of Pennsylvania; and, in my second year there, worked with Dr. Walter Hyde, head of the department of ancient history. Dr. Hyde lectured twice a week to about two hundred students, and I, the young assistant, had them for one hour a week in smaller sections. Dr. Hyde lectured on the rise of Christianity and took the agnostic position before the class. He spoke of the contradiction between Matthew's account of the genealogy of Jesus and that of Luke. I went to him after the class and told him that in the interest of truth he should be willing for me to present to the class the other view absolutely contrary to his own. Thus it was announced that the following week Dr. Hyde would give me one of his lecture periods, and I would answer the arguments against the historicity of the New Testament. The class included Jews, Catholics, Protestants, and agnostics, and considerable curiosity was shown as I announced my purpose to refute the arguments of my chief.

"First, I admitted definitely that there were two genealogies. The lines run parallel from Abraham to David, but then Matthew comes down to Jesus by way of Solomon the son of David, while Luke comes down to Jesus by way of Nathan the son of David. In others words, the two genealogies are the lines of two brothers, and the children become cousins. When I state that Luke's genealogy is that of the Virgin Mary and Matthew's genealogy is that of Joseph, I am not merely following the persistent tradition of the early church, as Dr. James Orr states it, but I am setting forth the only explanation that will fit the facts. The whole point of the difference is that Solomon's line was the royal line and Nathan's line was the legal line.

"For example, the former king of England had an older brother, now the Duke of Windsor, who had a prior claim to the throne of Britain. Suppose that Windsor had been the father of a son by a real queen before he abdicated. It can readily be seen that such a child might be a strong pretender to the throne in case there was no other heir apparent. George VI is in the royal line, for he has reigned; any children of Windsor might claim to be in a legal line. Nathan was the older brother of Solomon, but the younger brother took the throne. Nathan's line ran on through the years, and ultimately produced the Virgin Mary. Solomon's line ran on through the years and ultimately produced Joseph. Matthew does not say that Joseph begat Jesus (Matthew 1:16). And Luke uses a word for son that includes what we should call a son-in-law.

"But the greatest proof of all, lies in one of the names in the account of Matthew: the name Jechonias. It is that name that furnishes the reason for the inclusion of the genealogy of Jesus' stepfather, for it proves that Joseph could not have been the father of Jesus, or if he had been, that Jesus would not have been the Messiah. In the use of that name is conclusive evidence that Jesus is the son of Mary and not the son of Joseph. Jechonias was accursed of God with a curse that took the throne away from any of his descendants. 'Thus saith the Lord,' we read in Jeremiah 22:30, 'write ye this man childless, a man that shall not prosper in his days: for no man of his seed shall prosper, sitting upon the throne of David, and ruling any more in Judah.' Not one of the seven sons (I Chronicles 3:17, 18) of this man ever possessed the throne. No carnal son of this man could have been king because of the curse of God. If Jesus had been the son of Joseph, He would have been accursed and could never have been the Messiah.

"On the other hand, the line of Nathan was not the royal line. A son of Heli would have faced the fact that there was a regal line that would have contested any claim that came from the line of Nathan. How was the dilemma solved? It was solved in a manner that is so simple that it is the utter confusion of the agnostics who seek to tear thy Bible to pieces. The answer is this: The line that had no curse upon it produced Heli and his daughter the Virgin Mary and her Son Jesus Christ. He is therefore eligible by the line of Nathan and exhausts that line. The line that had a curse on it produced Joseph, exhausts the line of Solomon, for Joseph's other children now have an elder brother who, legally, by adoption, is the royal heir. How can the title be free in any case? A curse on one line and the lack of reigning royalty in the other.

"But when God the Holy Spirit begat the Lord Jesus in the womb of the Virgin without any use of a human father, the child that was born was the seed of David according to the flesh. And when Joseph married Mary and took the unborn child under his protecting care, giving Him the title that had come down to Him through His ancestor Solomon, the Lord Jesus became the legal Messiah, the royal Messiah, the uncursed Messiah, the true Messiah, the only possible Messiah. The lines are exhausted. Any man that ever comes into this world professing to fulfill the conditions will be a liar and the child of the Devil. The Lord Jesus announced that the attempt would be made; for describing the coming of the future Antichrist, the Saviour said, 'I am come in my Father's name, and ye receive me not: if another shall come in his own name, him ye will receive.' (John 5:43)"

What is the import of the doctrine of the Virgin Birth? Let us go back to Isaiah 53:9 for a starting point. In Isaiah 53:9 we read, "His grave (Christ's grave) was assigned to be with wicked men, yet with a rich man in His death; although He had done no violence, nor was there any deceit in His mouth." Here was a prophetic statement of the fact that Jesus Christ was going to be sinless. Do not miss that point if you got lost in the genealogy. Christ had to be sinless if He was to be our Messiah. He had to be blemishless. If He was tainted with a curse from the sperm of a human father, He could not possibly have gone to the cross as a sinless Messiah. Had that been the case, there could be no possible sacrifice for you and me. Now look at II Corinthians 5:21. This verse sheds a little more light upon this. "(God) He made Him who knew no sin to be sin on our behalf, that we might become the righteousness of God in Him." Christ knew no sin and there is no possible way to be reconciled to God outside of the sacrifice of Jesus Christ. Now this does not mean that Jesus Christ does not have an intellectual capacity to know what sin was. That is not what the Scriptures say. It means that He did not know it by experience. We know that to be true because Jesus knew enough about sin to talk about it and to reprove men for practicing it. Obviously He knew what it was, but He did not know it as a part of His character.

The sacrificial system that had been established in the Old Testament would bring any cursory reader of the Scriptures to at least one conclusion: the sacrifice had to be blemishless to be accepted. Whether it was a turtledove, or whether it was a goat or a calf or a bull, it could not have a defective ear, it could not have a scar on its leg, it had to be blemishless. God was preparing Israel to see that the Lamb of God who was to come would be blemishless. That does not mean that Jesus could not have a mole on His left cheek or a birthmark on His elbow. It meant that He could not be a sinner. He could not be tainted with human depravity.

Look at Hebrews 4:15. "For we do not have a high priest who cannot sympathize with our weaknesses, but one who has been tempted in all things as we are, yet without sin." This does not mean that Jesus Christ was tempted in everything that you and I are tempted in. It means that He was tempted in all points of *His* nature, just as you and I are tempted in all points of our nature. Let me illustrate that. Our temptations come from three sources: the world, the flesh, and the devil. But Christ's temptations are different from ours in that His nature is different from ours. In other words, He was never tempted to despair after defeat, because He never knew defeat. He was never tempted to tell a second lie to cover up the first lie because there was no sin in Him. And you say, "Well, what does the Scripture mean then, when it says He was tempted in all points as we?" It means that He was tempted to do things which were in His power to do, but which He did not do. This point was driven home to me soundly when Dr. Bruce Metzger got to this point in his exposition. He said, "I want to see a show of hands of everyone who has been tempted to turn stone into bread." And of course, no one put his hands up. It is not within our power to change stones into bread, but it was within Christ's power. It was within Christ's power to dispute Pilate. It was within His power to come off the cross, as He was taunted to do. So when the Scriptures say that we do not have an unsympathetic high priest, do not doubt it on the basis that Christ never knew what it was to have a wife walk out of the house. Do not feel that He does not understand your problem if you have a sick child and He never had any children. The Scriptures teach that in all points of His divine nature, He was tempted to the fullest degree, just as we in our human and depraved nature are tempted to our fullest degree. Therefore, He is sympathetic because He has been fully pushed to the limit of His capacity and knows your predicament when you are pushed to the edge.

In Hebrews 2:17, 18 we learn something else about the sinless nature of Jesus Christ. "Therefore, He had to be made like His brethren in all things, that He might become a merciful and faithful high priest in things pertaining to God, to make propitiation for the sins of the people. For since He Himself was tempted in that which He has suffered, He is able to come to the aid of those who are tempted." Our predicament is different from Christ's. Our predicament is different from that of the angels. We are not tempted as Christ was tempted, but yet we are not left with a high priest who does not know what it is to have a headache. Jesus Christ was tempted fully and He knows what it means to be pushed to the limit of your capacity. Now look again in Hewbrews 9:11-14. "But when Christ appeared as a high priest of the good things to come, He entered through the greater and more perfect tabernacle, not made with hands, that is to say, not of this creation; and not through the blood of goats and calves, but through His own blood, He entered the holy place once for all, having obtained eternal redemption. For if the blood of goats and bulls and the ashes of a heifer sprinkling those who have been defiled, sanctify for the cleansing of the flesh, how much more will the blood of Christ, who through the eternal Spirit offered Himself without blemish to God, cleanse your conscience from dead works to serve the living God?" Now that is marvelous. The important part of this passage, I believe, is what we read there in the last verse, 14. "He offered Himself without blemish to God." But you see, if Joseph had fathered Christ, He would have been spotted with the blemish of human depravity. He would have been like you and me. He could have been a liar, a cheater, a murderer, and when Jesus said out of the heart of man comes evil things, fornication, murders, adultery, he would have had to have been talking about Himself also, had He not been born of a virgin by the supernatural conception of the Holy Spirit.

All history points to the cross of Christ. And all the prophecies of the Old Testament and the teachings of the New Testament epistles make it clear that the individual who was nailed to that cross had to be blemishless if He was to be a sacrifice as God had commanded. Now if you deny the fact that Jesus Christ was born of a virgin, then you deny the fact that He was sinless. And if you are satisfied with a sinful Messiah, you are resting in no messiah at all. God had said all throughout the Old Testament, it has to be a blemishless sacrifice, and how could God have possibly taken Christ's death as our substitute? He could not. But if Jesus Christ was not the Messiah, we never will see the Messiah, because the genealogies teach us that Christ exhausted both lines. We are never going to have it again. It is not going to pass through history again. One of the evangelical reasons for studying this passage is that if you have a Roman Catholic friend or neighbor, here is a place where you can open the Scriptures to him. "Do you believe in the Virgin Birth? Now, let us talk about what that really means for us". Instead of getting sidetracked to Mary, let us get sidetracked to where it would lead us if Christ was not sinless.

There is a great chasm that rests between man and God. It has been bridged by the Lord Jesus Christ, but the bridge would have been blown to bits, had there been one slip up in the character of the Lord Jesus Christ, or the case would have been if he had been fathered by someone just as sinful as you and me. How marvelous is God's Word. How marvelous are these difficult-to-read genealogies. How important they are!

"SUFFERED UNDER PONTIUS PILATE"
John 18:28-40

The importance of this phrase is that God the Father wants us to know that Jesus Christ was deliberately delivered unto a Gentile procurator after He had been delivered unto the Jews, both of whom could not substantiate any real accusation against Him. It was so that the Scriptures might be fulfilled that He went to the slaughter as a lamb, unblemished, unstained, and of His own will. He bore our sins, but He had no sin in Him. He had done no wrong. The conversation between Christ and Pilate in the verses shows us just that. Verses 28-40 of John 18 read, "They led Jesus therefore from Caiaphas into the Praetorium; and it was early; (before dawn) and they themselves did not enter into the Praetorium in order that they might not be defiled, but might eat the Passover. Pilate therefore went out to them, and said, 'What accusation do you bring against this Man?' They answered and said to him, 'If this Man were not an evildoer, we would not have delivered Him up to you.' Pilate therefore said to them, 'Take Him yourselves, and judge Him according to your law.' The Jews said to him, 'We are not permitted to put any one to death,' that the word of Jesus might be fulfilled, which He spoke, signifying by what kind of death He was about to die.

"Pilate therefore entered again into the Praetorium, and summoned Jesus, and said to Him, 'You are the King of the Jews?' Jesus answered, 'Are you saying this on your own initiative, or did others tell you about Me?' Pilate answered, 'I am not a Jew, am I? Your own nation and the chief priests delivered You up to me; what have You done?' Jesus answered, 'My kingdom is not of this world. If My kingdom were of this world, then My servants would be fighting, that I might not be delivered up to the Jews; but as it is, My kingdom is not of this realm.' Pilate therefore said to Him, 'So You are a king?' Jesus answered, 'You say correctly that I am a king. For this I have been born, and for this I have come into the world, to bear witness to the truth. Every one who is of the truth hears My voice.' Pilate said to Him, 'What is truth?'

"And when he had said this, he went out again to the Jews, and said to them, 'I find no guilt in Him. But you have a custom, that I should release someone for you at the Passover; do you wish then that I release for you the King of the Jews?' Therefore they cried out again, saying, 'Not this Man, but Barabbas.' Now Barabbas was a robber."

There are seven sections of study connected to this passage. Number one, Jesus Christ is brought to Pilate's court in verse 28. Second, in verses 29 and 30, Pilate demands a formal charge. Third, in verses 31 and 32, Pilate shirks his responsibility. Fourth, Pilate examines Christ from verses 33 to 37. Fifth, Pilate finds Him innocent in verse 38. Six, Pilate attempts a compromise in verse 39, and seven, Pilate utterly fails to do what he started out to do, and that was to exonerate Christ in the midst of the Jews.

Number one, then, Jesus Christ was brought into Pilate's court. Who was this man Pilate? Pilate was under the authority of Rome as a Roman procurator. He had been sent to this part of Palestine to rule for Caesar. But as a governor, he was a flop. He made a number of bad, political bungles with the Jews in Jerusalem which got him off on the wrong foot. The first was that when he took power, he went about the city of Jerusalem setting up icons of past Roman emperors. The Jews revolted against that, and there was such an uproar that he had to take them down. Second, he wanted to build a new and better aqueduct to bring water into the city more easily from the northern parts of Galilee. Where did he get the money to do it? He went to the Jewish temple and raided their treasury to build his aqueduct. Needless to say, that angered the Jews. The third stupid thing he did was to take metal shields and paint upon them the insignia of the Emperor in Rome and have them put on sticks over the ramparts of the city wall. It caused another riot, and once again, not only did he back down, but he got a direct order from the Emperor to take them down and not put them up again. So, Jesus met Pilate the bungler. This was the buffoon who was now standing before the Lord of Grace. I do not believe that any of us really are capable of gleaning the rich meat that is here; nevertheless, it is here for us to study.

One of the most horrific perversions of justice in Jewish history had just taken place. Jesus had been illegally arrested. He had not been charged with a crime before He got into the basement of Caiaphas' house that evening, and Annas, the high priest, could not substantiate the accusations that the Jews brought against Jesus. Despite that they brought Him to Pilate. There is a very interesting thing to be noted in verse 28. "They led Jesus therefore from Caiaphas into the Praetorium; and it was early; and they themselves did not enter into the Praetorium in order that they might not be defiled, but might eat the Passover." You have to understand the racial hatred between Jews and Gentiles that existed here. The Jews wanted to have Jesus murdered, but they would not dare go into the Praetorium to pollute themselves, because if they polluted themselves, they would not have time to go home and go through all of the cleansing processes so that they would be able to take the Passover feast the next day. Such was their dilemma. Jesus is in Pilate's court and it is early in the morning. We read in verse 30, "Well, do you think we would have brought Him to you if He didn't do something wrong?" You just do not wake up the Roman procurator of Palestine at four o'clock in the morning! But that is what these people were doing. Half of the Sanhedrin was there with Jesus presenting Him before Pilate.

Secondly, Pilate demands a formal charge. In verse 30 he says, "What accusation do you bring against this Man?" He demanded a formal charge, but he did not get one. Why did he not get one? The Jews knew they had no evidence, and you cannot present a formal charge against a man if there is no evidence. They could not get anything out of Him, so what were they going to tell this Gentile procurator? "This Man claims to be God?", Pilate would have said. "So we have a lot of nuts running around; take Him and judge Him by your own laws." Because they had no evidence against Him, no formal charge was made. Pilate's words in these two verses show three elements of the Roman Law. The first is that a specific charge has to be made. Second, the accusers have to be present. You could not tie a man up and throw him to the jailer without a charge and witness. The accusers had to be there and they had to be there with a formal charge. The third thing was that the defendant was allowed to defend himself. He could do without having to hire someone to defend him. Now, if you will look at Luke 23:2, you will see that they would have Pilate believe that they never would have arrested an innocent man. This is very interesting to me. First of all we note the hypocrisy that we see among the Sanhedrin. But their arrogance manifests itself when they say, "Do you think that we would have brought somebody to you who hadn't done something that was very bad?" Of course that question never was answered. Luke 23:2 reads, "And they began to accuse Him, saying, 'We found this man misleading our nation and forbidding to pay taxes to Caesar, and saying that He Himself is Christ, a King." Well, anybody who had been with Jesus in His earthly ministry knew that Jesus was not a seditionist. In fact, He had told them to stop begrudging the fact that Rome was collecting taxes! Pilate might even have heard that Jesus had said those things.

We come now to the third section. Pilate shirks off his responsibility in verses 31 and 32. Here is a man who we must assume was fairly bright, or he would not have been in this position. Yet, perhaps we should not make that assumption because there are many people in high offices today who are not bright. "Pilate therefore said to them, 'Take Him yourselves, and judge Him according to your law.' The Jews said to him, 'We are not permitted to put anyone to death.' " Now do you see that there is a missing link there? He said, "Take Him and judge Him according to your law," but they said, "We are not allowed to put anyone to death." What is missing here is that they did not say to Pilate, "We already have accused Him of blasphemy," which would not have made any sense to Pilate, who would not have cared either. So, that missing link is never mentioned. Pilate would not understand or appreciate it, and the Jews knew it, so they just skip over that part and say, "Well, we are not permitted to put anyone to death, Pilate. We want you to kill Him." It put Pilate in the position of having to examine Jesus, which of course was their whole purpose.

Pilate's real character emerges here. I do not know how you picture this man, but I see him as a vacillating, shrewd and confused man. His wife had said to him, "Don't have anything to do with this man." He did not listen to his wife. He came to Jesus assuming Him innocent and he found this to be true, as far as Roman law was concerned; but the Jews were at the gates, pressing him hard for an accusation. He had to now find out why He was worthy of death, if He was guilty at all. There is a curious passage in Acts 4:27, 28. "For truly in this city there were gathered together against Thy holy servant Jesus, whom Thou didst annoint, both Herod and Pontius Pilate, along with the Gentiles and the peoples of Israel, to do whatever Thy hand and Thy purpose predestined to occur." It was foreordained of God for Christ to be tried, to be killed, to be buried, and to rise again on the third day. Now you say to me, "Why is it so important that it was predestined? Didn't it happen?" It is very important to know that it was predestined because it teaches us that God is in control of history and that God is in control of our salvation. There was no way Christ was not going to go to the cross. There was no way He was not going to be charged falsely by the Sanhedrin. There was no way He was not going to be found innocent by Pilate, so that the Scriptures might be fulfilled. That God's Word is to be manifested as true according to prophecy, is very important to God. Prophecy must come true if God is to be shown to be God. The only way that you know that God is a God of history is that what He tells you is going to happen takes place, right down to the smallest detail.

Now let us go to the fourth section. Verses 33-37 show Pilate's examination of Jesus Christ. There is another gross injustice here because Pilate was examining Jesus Christ not as a rebellious Jew, which in the eyes of some He may have been, but He was examining Him as an enemy to Caesar. Where Pilate could possibly come up with that charge is not said. Any Roman procurator would have to investigate a charge like that, even though unsubstantiated. Pilate knew that the envy of the Sanhedrin was what had brought Jesus to him. It is recorded in Matthew 27:18 that it was envy that moved the Sanhedrin to arrest Christ. Envy! Pilate must have heard of Jesus Christ before he met Him here, the great teacher and healer of Nazareth. Certainly the story of Bartimeus in Jericho being healed must have been known. He certainly knew that Christ had entered into the city just a few days before on the colt of an ass as a victorious King as the people cried out, "Hosannah!" Certainly that came to his attention. But even with all of those things he asked Jesus Christ, in verse 33, "Are You the King of the Jews?" Jesus, in effect, answered him and said, "Now Pilate, are you saying this or asking this on your own initiative? Is there something in Me that you see now that provokes that question or has someone else told you about Me?" I believe that Jesus Christ, at this point, was addressing Pilate's conscience. He was saying, "Pilate, be honest with Me. Do you really want some information or are you trying to get off the hook with the Jews outside your door here who are so self-righteous that they can not even come in here and accuse Me themselves because they don't want to get themselves dirty." He put his conscience on the line. Pilate did not answer the question. But we do know this; that if by the word "King" Pilate thought Him to be a rival to Caesar, he would have known, had Jesus Christ chosen to defend Himself on that basis, that He was not an enemy of Caesar. In fact, we find an interesting verse in John 6:15 that is very descriptive of Christ's attitude. John 6:15 says, "Jesus therefore perceiving that they were intending to come and take Him by force, to make Him king, withdrew again to the mountain by Himself alone." He did not want to be made king! Why did He not want to be made king? Because He knew that the kingdom which He was to rule was not an earthly kingdom. So what would be the point of riding a horse and wearing a crown? He knew that the Jews did not understand that. He knew most of them would reject Him on that basis, and now Pilate says to Him, "Are You a King?" Jesus has left Pilate absolutely breathless as far as any accusation goes. There is nothing that proceeds from the mouth of the Son of God which gives Pilate anything to say against Him as far as accusing Him of being an evildoer.

We come now to the most important part of this entire text. It is where Jesus tells Pilate why He came to this earth. We read in verse 36, "Jesus answered, 'My kingdom is not of this world." The preposition "of" is extremely important. Had He said, "My kingdom is not in this world," that would have meant something completely different. And note also that He says, "If My kingdom were of this world, then My servants would be fighting." Jesus was not a pacifist. If it had been His will to conquer what He knew had to be conquered, He would have done it with a sword. Once the Jews had rejected Him, He is able to say that He is a King.

Note Pilate's change of attitude from verse 33-37. "Pilate therefore said to Him, 'Are you the king of the Jews?' " And in 37 he said, "So You are a King?" Now where did he get his evidence to conclude that? There was only one possible way, and it was done in a negative way. Because there was nothing in Jesus that he could fault, he concluded that what Jesus had said about His identity was true and that the Sanhedrin was wrong. But Pilate is a professional politician. And professional politicians do not stand on what they know to be right if it will cost them popularity. Pilate was no exception and so he compromised himself.

This compromise is what brings us to the fifth section. Pilate has said to Jesus Christ, in verse 38, "What is truth?" Now that verse itself has been taken out of context by many and has been spoken about philosophical truth. I want you to see it in relation to what just precedes it. In effect Jesus was saying, "Pilate, I've come to this earth to bear witness to the Father who sent Me." And Pilate missed it completely and asked. "What is truth?" That tells us that Pilate was not one of God's people. Why could Pilate not understand who Jesus was? There He was, standing right in front of him. You say, "If the Son of God was to stand in front of me, I'd know Who He was." Would you? Pilate did not. How is it that men can be confronted by the Son of God in the Gospel and not know it? How can people hear the Gospel of Christ preached week after week and still not know who He is? The answer is that "The natural man does not accept the things of the Spirit of God; for they are foolishness to him, and he cannot understand them because they are spiritually appraised." (I Corinthians 2:14) Are you spiritually appraised? Or would you, along with Pilate, ask of Jesus Christ, "What is truth?"

Now look at Pilate's deadly compromise at our sixth point in verse 39, "But you have a custom, that I should release someone for you at the Passover; do you wish then that I release for you the King of the Jews?" I believe he is mocking Christ here at this point. He knew He was innocent. He said, "I find no guilt in this man." What did he do? In an instant, he made an assessment of whom he was going to have to face if he did not give in to the Jews. He thought, "I am a Roman procurator. My job will be gone if I do not satisfy these Jews. What if they cause a riot? I have already bungled these people three times. I put images up, I had to take them down. I raided their treasuries to build an aqueduct and then I went and put those shields up and Caesar said, 'Take them down,' Oh, I've been made to look bad in front of these people and one more time and they may send me home." Pilate was more interested in the praise of men than in what he knew to be right. To compromise your conscience is the most awful thing that you can do in life. To know what is right and yet to say, "But I am going to go in this direction," is compromising your conscience. Pilate in my eyes is the greatest loser in all history. How many men have had the privilege of standing before God Almighty and hearing Him tell him who He was and why He came to this earth and miss the point? Well, Pilate not only did not recognize Him, but he compromised his conscience and he went down in history as the professional politician "par excellance."

In conclusion, what does this mean for you and me? You also have to come to a conclusion about Jesus Christ. You have to admit He was either insane, or that He was a charlatan, or that He was God. Which is it? Was He from heaven or was He from hell? Some thought He was from hell. They said, "He casts out demons, He must have demonic power." The punch here is in verse 37. You see, the believer is never afraid of the truth, but the unbeliever is. I was talking to a lady who is not a

Christian. I talked with her for forty minutes about the Gospel of Christ. She just would not hear anything about the truth because she did not want to. As I pressed truth on her, she avoided it. Truth condemns, and those who do not know the truth and do not want to hear the truth will never know it. But if you hear Christ's voice, you also hear the truth. You know what truth is because you know Christ. Men did not believe that the earth rotated around the sun. They said, "It can't be true." Jesus said, "I am the way, the truth and the life; no man can come unto the Father but by Me," and men say, "It can't be true." God says, "All have sinned and fallen short of the glory of God." And men say, "That can't be true." Some believe it and some still say it cannot be true. What do you say?

"WAS CRUCIFIED, DEAD, AND BURIED"
Romans 5:6

In August of 1967 my wife and I were in a very serious automobile accident that was fatal to one of the passengers. I had the experience twice that night of regaining my consciousness from a state that was somewhat less than that. The first was when I struggled out of the automobile, and the second was after I had got to the hospital that night and had been given an injection which put me into outer space. I remember waking from that in a very groggy and sluggish state of mind. That sense of sluggishness illustrates the text of Romans 5:6. "For while we were still helpless, (sluggish) at the right time Christ died for the ungodly." This word in the Greek means weak, feeble, slow, sluggish. Here is a description of the spiritual state of the natural man before he becomes aware of what God has done for him in Christ.

Now if it is impossible for man to do anything for himself, which we know to be true regarding salvation, then we need to look at the two kinds of impossibilities which we know about in this life. There are conditional impossibilities and there are unconditional possibilities. Let me give you an illustration of a conditional impossibility. Harry Jones is a cripple. I say of Harry, "Harry cannot get up and walk across the room unless something happens to his legs." That is a conditional impossibility. Unless the conditions change he can't walk. An unconditional impossibility or possibility would be illustrated by the statement, "It is impossible for something to exist and not to exist simultaneously." That is an unconditional impossibility because no matter what you do to the conditions, something cannot exist and not exist at the same time simultaneously. That brings us to a deeper understanding of the text as regards the word "helpless". This is a conditional impossibility. Man, by his own nature, cannot help himself regarding salvation. So it is impossible for man to be saved unless the condition changes. The conditional change is that God has provided a way for man's salvation through Jesus Christ's incarnation, death and resurrection. Let us look at four things. First, man's impotence before God; second, that Christ died on schedule; third, that it was Christ's death that saved us; and fourth, that He died for us while we were helpless, not when we were ready.

First, let us examine some verses in Scripture which speak about man's impotence before God. John 3:3 says: "Jesus answered and said to him, 'Truly, truly, I say to you, unless one is born again, he cannot see the kingdom of God.'" Then we turn to John 8:43 where we read: "Why do you not understand what I am saying? It is because you cannot hear My Word." Then read John 14:16, 17: "And I will ask the Father, and He will give you another Helper, that He may be with you forever; that is the Spirit of truth, whom the world cannot receive, because it does not behold Him or know Him, but you know Him because He abides with you, and will be in you." And finally, Romans 8:7, 8 reads: "Because the mind set on the flesh is hostile toward God for it does not subject itself to the law of God, for it is not even able to do so; and those who are in the flesh cannot please God." When you take those four passages and couple them with I Corinthians 2:14, we have a clear picture of man's impotence before God. This is something that you and I need to know in our evangelism. When we talk to someone about the Lord Jesus Christ, and try to explain the way of salvation to them over and over and over again and it seems to fall on deaf ears, it is not because you lack wisdom or faith, but until the Spirit of God awakens a man he cannot see the kingdom of God, he cannot hear God's Word, he cannot receive the things of the Spirit, he cannot subject himself to the law of God, he cannot please God, he cannot cease from his sins. If I gave you a radio which did not have a receiver in it, it would be of no value to you. I could broadcast waves toward that radio but until a receiver is put in the radio, the message will not be perceived. The Gospel of Christ is passed out over the airwaves and the pulpits of this world to millions of ears. Some ears receive it, some ears do not receive it. The ears that do not receive it are the ears that do not have the receiver. God has not naturally placed in the mind of man the spiritual discernment that it takes to understand the teaching of the Scriptures. This does not mean that just because a man does not have a receiver at the age of 20 that he will go through his entire life without the receiver. It is God's timing as to when the Spirit gives us the ability to perceive spiritual teaching. We see from this, then, that man is helpless.

The second important part of the text is that Christ died on schedule. We must not forget that God is not bound by time. He lives and dwells in eternity. You and I, as His creatures are bound by time which means that the things that God does in history are not perceptible to us sometimes because we expect God to work on a timetable of "time", when He operates from eternity. If God has decreed that an event shall take place at a point in history, that is when it will take place. A thousand years is as a day to God. He does not measure time as we do. We get very anxious about God not doing some things. We see someone we love who is not yet a believer and we get anxious. Yet, God has it all in hand.

Christ's arrival at Bethlehem was not one minute early or one minute late, according to prophecy. In Isaiah 55:8, 9 we read: " 'For My thoughts are not your thoughts, neither are your ways My ways,' declares the Lord. 'For as the heavens are higher than the earth, so are My ways higher than your ways, and My thoughts than your thoughts.' " When we talk about the Lord ordaining a specific date for the Lord Jesus Christ to come to earth, and for the miracle of the incarnation to take place, that is not just another event which has to take place on schedule. One French theologian said, "Christ died at a decisive moment." That is false. Christ did not die at a decisive moment, because it implies that Christ decided that on that particular day His life should come to an end and He should sacrifice Himself. Rather, it was a preordained moment! We read in Acts 2:23, "This Man, delivered up by the predetermined plan and foreknowledge of God, you nailed to a cross by the hands of godless men and put Him to death." Because God's decrees are eternal, there are no variables which can affect His decisions. Most Christians think He reacts to history. Rather, He controls it, and history reacts to God's eternal decrees.

Furthermore, because God is perfect, we know that Christ died at the precise moment. Let us see what Scripture says in Revelation 13:8. "And all who dwell on the earth will worship him, every one whose name has not been written from the foundation of the world in the book of life of the Lamb who has been slain." Note that the "Lamb" of God had been slain in God's eyes long before history began as you and I know it. If you understand that particular teaching, it is a mark of a mature Christian because it means you have been studying the Word of God enough to know that if God is not bound by time, His eternal decrees are as good as accomplished even before they have been accomplished. Ephesians 1:4, 5 reads: "Just as He chose us in Him before the foundation of the world, that we should be holy and blameless before Him. In love He predestined us to adoption as sons through Jesus Christ to Himself, according to the kind intention of His will." Now drop your eyes down to verse 11; "Also we have obtained an inheritance, having been predestined according to His purpose who works all things after the counsel of His will." *When God calls a meeting,* there is nobody there but God. His own will is the only thing that comes into play. Now turn to Galatians 4:4; "But when the fulness of the time came, God sent forth His Son, born of a woman, born under the Law." You see, there was to be no mistake about it. It had to be at a particular time. Do you ask "Why?" First of all, Jesus Christ's death was eternally planned. Second, the Old Testament has set it down in great detail. Third, Jesus Christ arrived at Bethlehem on schedule.

In the 17th century there was a British astronomer by the

name of Edmund Halley. Halley had been studying Newton's law of physics, gravity and mathematics for some time. The comet that came past this particular point of our solar system in 1682 Halley figured to return in 1757. It did, but he died fifteen years before it returned. It was named Halley's Comet, after the man who predicted it would return in a specific year. How did he arrive at the conclusion that it would come when it did? He worked on the basis of Newton's math, physics, gravity, etc. Above all else, the arrival of Halley's Comet the second time proved that Newton was right about his mathematics. If Newton's laws can be relied upon to predict the arrival of a comet, then if Jesus Christ arrives in Bethlehem on schedule as it was predicted in the Old Testament, does that not tell us something about the basis of God's Word? If you have a God that makes predictions which do not come true, you do not have a God. Before Jesus Christ's incarnation, many people looked forward to the arrival. Just think of the excitement in 1757. Halley had been dead for fifteen years. People were waiting to see whether Halley's Comet would appear. Then it arrived. Christ was born according to prophecy; Christ went to the cross according to the Scriptures; He died according to the Scriptures; He was buried according to the Scriptures, and He was raised according to the Scriptures. All that tells you and me is that when God says something He means it, because His prophecies always come true. The Old Testament believers were vindicated forever, just as Edmund Halley was vindicated forever.

Now, this "due time" that we read about in Romans 5:6 also has something to do with secular history. This is an extremely important passage for me, personally. It tells us something about the clock that had wound down to a stop from both Greek and Roman cultures. The greatest historical period of thought had passed. We read in I Corinthians 1:21 about the condition of the philosophical world at that time. Do you know what it was? It was foolish. Paul says this in I Corinthians 1:21, "For since in the wisdom of God the world through its wisdom did not come to know God, God was well-pleased through the foolishness of the message preached to save those who believe." Do you know what that means? It means that Sophicles had come and gone. Aristotle had come and gone. Plato had come and gone. All of the culture and intellectual powers of the Assyrians had risen and waned. Egypt had risen and waned, never to rise again as a material power. Babylon had risen and waned. Greece had risen and waned. Rome was on the way down when Paul wrote this letter. The world's wisdom was on the table and God confounded it and showed it to be foolishness by the message of the Gospel of Christ. Do not think that we live on the bright side of intellectualism in the world. We do not. We live on the dark side of it. The intellectual and philosophical exponents of this world were already gone before Christ came. When Christ came, He came on time. When all the philosophers of the world had said all they had to say, Christ came. How did God confound their wisdom? By preaching a message which all unbelievers call foolishness.

The third point is that we are saved by Christ's life. Christ was only able to offer us the sacrifice that God demanded by dying. God the Father was not looking for a sacrifice of teaching. He was not looking for a sacrifice of example. "Christ died as our example, suffer and you'll make it." You do not find that in the Scriptures. We are saved by His death and nothing else.

Now finally, the fourth point finds itself imbedded in a verse just two verses down from the text. Look at Romans 5:6, 7, 8. "For while we were still helpless, at the right time Christ died for the ungodly. For one will hardly die for a righteous man; though perhaps for the good man someone would dare even to die. But God demonstrates His own love toward us, in that while we were yet sinners, Christ died for us." God does not wait for the world to rise to His level, because it cannot. God condescends to our level, judges it and says there is no way to reach His level except through Christ. Christ died for us while we were yet sinners. Now what do you think that verse 7 means? Let me contrast the highest level of man's love with God's love. There is a mine disaster in West Virginia. One of the pillars has given way and there has been an explosion and poisonous gas is being breathed throughout the tunnels of this underground mine. The mask of one of the men has been torn and he is not able to use it to filter out the poisonous gas. Here is another man and he is not married and has no children. He comes to his friend and says, "Look, you've got a wife, you've got children, you take my mask, because they need you and I don't have anybody up there waiting for me." Most men are touched with that, and they say, "Isn't that wonderful? That is the highest sacrifice that a man can make for another man." And I agree with you. It is the highest sacrifice a *man* can make for another man. But it does not illustrate God's love for us. Christ has come to us and laid down His life for us, but He is now alive. We were saved by His death, and are preserved by His resurrection.

The wisdom of God in the proclamation of the Gospel confounds the wisdom of the world. How does it do that? Because it takes the very best that man can offer and exposes it as non-productive. Is that not the best way to show that something is worthless? The Gospel of Christ confounds the wisdom of this world because it is foolishness, and how wonderful to be saved by God's foolishness! That is the wisdom of God. He saves us through the foolish preaching of the Gospel. Are you still helpless? There is only one thing you need to do if you are helpless, and that is to throw your helplessness onto Christ. Let His wisdom confound your wisdom. Be saved by foolishness, go down, bend the knee, and ask Christ to reveal these things to you. "For God so loved the world, that He gave His only begotten Son, that whoever believes in Him should not perish, but have eternal life." (John 3:16).

"HE DESCENDED INTO HELL"
I Peter 3:18-20

We come now to the most controversial section of the Creed. Controversial because some have omitted it and others have misinterpreted this section. Let us look briefly at the two major misinterpretations of what we mean when we say, "He descended into Hell." The first is that Christ went there to suffer. Christ did not go to Hell to suffer. Christ suffered on the cross all He was ordained to suffer. There are a number of reasons why that is so, but I will mention only one of them. Jesus Christ said on the cross, "It is finished." He did not say, "It's almost over." God had turned His back on His Son where He separated Himself from His Son as Christ bore the entire weight of God's wrath which should have fallen upon you and me. It is misunderstood that God had His back turned toward His Son throughout the three days and the three nights that He was in the belly of the earth. That is just not so. The second misinterpretation is that Jesus Christ's victory over the grave is manifested not in the resurrection, but in His presence in hell. That is also false. God says in the Scriptures that He raised Christ from the dead and in the resurrection He has victory over the grave.

Well, then, why did Christ go to Hell? The first answer to

that question is that He went there to fulfill both prophecy and history. Turn to Matthew 12:40 and you will see there a verse that has a definite connection to one in the Old Testament which we need to turn to also. In Matthew 12:40 Jesus says, "An evil and adulterous generation craves for a sign; and yet no sign shall be given to it but the sign of Jonah the prophet; for just as Jonah was three days and three nights in the belly of a sea monster, so shall the Son of Man be three days and three nights in the heart of the earth." In conjunction with that read Jonah 2:2 and let us find out what it is that Christ is saying concerning Jonah. Jonah died, and Jonah was raised from the dead. Jonah did not go into some kind of unconcious state in the fish only to be resuscitated after three days and three nights. He died, and we know it from what we read here in Jonah 2:2, "I called out of my distress to the Lord, and He answered me. I cried for help from the depth of Sheol; thou didst hear my voice."

What is interesting about that is found in two things. First, Jesus Christ identifies His presence in Sheol (Hell) three days and three nights, with the fact that Jonah was there three days and three nights. You see, they had all been asking for a sign, "Show us, prove to us that you are the Son of God." He says, "An evil generation wants a sign, I'm only going to give you one sign, the sign is that of Jonah, just as he was three days in Sheol, so will I be." It speaks of the fact that God's Son identifies Himself with Jonah's historical death and resurrection. It is not a small mistake to maintain that Jonah did not really die. Because if Jonah did not die, then the prophecy, historically speaking, of Matthew 12:40 implies that Christ did not really die. He suffered, yes, then went into some kind of a quasi-limbo somewhere and did not really die.

With those two things in mind, turn to I Peter 3:18, 20. "For Christ also died for sins once for all, the just for the unjust, in order that He might bring us to God, having been put to death in the flesh, but made alive in the Spirit; in which (refers to the Spirit) also He went and made proclamation to the spirits now in prison, who once were disobedient, when the patience of God kept waiting in the days of Noah, during the construction of the ark, in which a few, that is, eight persons, were brought safely through the water." Now that does not explain the whole mystery to us in those verses, but it does tell us this: In the spirit, after His death, before He was bodily raised, Christ went to make proclamation to some disobedient spirits who were imprisoned in hell. But we cannot just leave it there because the Scripture expounds to us more clearly what hell looked like and what it was composed of. To remove the cobwebs, we need to turn to Luke 16. The word Sheol is simply the Hebrew word for the place to which all of the dead went. The Greek word, Hades, came out of the word Sheol and our present word Hell from Hades. There were two sections of this Sheol. One of them was a nice place to be and one of them was a bad place to be. Look at the parable of the rich man and Lazarus as it is seen in Luke 16:19. "Now there was a certain rich man, and he habitually dressed in purple and fine linen, gaily living in splendor every day. And a certain poor man named Lazarus was laid at his gate, covered with sores, and longing to be fed with the crumbs which were falling from the rich man's table; besides, even the dogs were coming and licking his sores. Now it came about that the poor man died and he was carried away by the angels to Abraham's bosom; and the rich man also died and was buried. And in Hades he lifted up his eyes, being in torment, and saw Abraham far away, and Lazarus in his bosom. And he cried out and said, 'Father Abraham, have mercy on me and send Lazarus, that he may dip the tip of his finger in water and cool off my tongue; for I am in agony in this flame.' But Abraham said, 'Child, remember that during your life you received your good things, and likewise Lazarus bad things; but now he is being comforted here, and you are in agony. And besides all this, between us and you there is a great chasm fixed, in order that those who wish to come over from here to you may not be able, and that none may cross over from there to us.' " Now, in light of what we have read in I Peter 3, we have seen that Jesus Christ, in the Spirit, descended to wherever these spirits were imprisoned. These are the spirits, these fallen sons of God, of Genesis 6, that came to the earth to have intercourse with the daughters of men, and attempted to populate the earth with some kind of a deformed human being. That was cut short by the flood. There were other people there also because Sheol was divided into two parts. It included everyone who died in the Old Testament economy. The believers, those who were justified by faith, went to what Christ called Abraham's bosom. The non-believer went to what is known as the place of torment. So there are two places within one compound in what the Old Testament knew as the after life. Note in verse 19 of I Peter 3 that Jesus went to make a proclamation to these disobedient spirits. What did He say to them? He did not come to preach salvation, as though they might have a second chance. He came to proclaim, herald, or shout victory. He is not shouting victory for them, but He was shouting victory for Himself in that the redemption of the believers had just taken place, but that their doom was sealed.

Now, He went also to preach to the dead in Christ. If you will just drop your eye down the page to I Peter 4:6, you will read: "For the gospel has for this purpose been preached even to those who are dead, that though they are judged in the flesh as men, they may live in the spirit according to the will of God." What did Jesus say to the thief on the cross who believed in Him? He said, "Today, you will be with Me in Paradise." That tells us three things. It was going to happen that day, it was going to be in a place called Paradise, (Abraham's bosom) and third, that Christ and this man were going to be together. So we know Christ was alive and we know He was with the saints, as they had been gathered for centuries in this category of Sheol known as Abraham's bosom. When we press this a little bit farther, we will see that it makes clear that Jesus Christ spent those three days and three nights after the cross, proclaiming and preaching in two different directions to two different groups of people in Sheol.

Some use Psalm 16:10 to try to prove that Jesus Christ did not go to hell for this reason or for any other reason. If you will study the context, you will see that it is mistaken. Psalm 16:10 reads: "For Thou wilt not abandon my soul to Sheol; neither wilt Thou allow Thy Holy One (a reference to the Messiah) to see the pit." That does not mean that Jesus Christ did not go to Sheol; it means that it was not able to hold Him. Death did not have a power over Christ. One of the benefits for us in the crucifixion and the resurrection is that our last enemy, which is death itself, has been crushed by Christ.

Now someone may say, "Why were there any human

spirits in Abraham's bosom anyway? Didn't all the believers go to be in heaven in the Old Testament as soon as they died?" No, they did not. And the sharp, critical student of the Scriptures should know why. Why were not the Old Testament believers in heaven when they died? Because there had been no procurement of a ransom yet. Christ had not redeemed anybody in the Old Testament. That act in history had not yet come. And even though the Old Testament believers were justified by faith in the Messiah to come, the redemption had not yet taken place. So, heaven at that point was empty of regenerate souls. Until the redemption was secured, there could be no one facing an almighty and holy God in His heaven. Until the cross of Christ, there were those who were justified by faith, but there was no one who was redeemed. Abraham believed and it was reckoned to him as righteousness. Moses believed, and it was accounted to him as righteousness. David believed and it was accounted to him as righteousness. But none of them had been redeemed. So they went to Sheol; not to suffer, but to be in bliss until the Messiah that they did believe was coming, came. When He came, He descended into hell to preach to them the fact that their faith had not been in vain and that Christ's presence there after the cross vindicated them forever. The greatest rescue mission ever took place between I Peter 3 and Ephesians 4, which I will ask you to turn to at this point.

This brings us to the last reason why Jesus Christ went to hell. He went there to proclaim damnation to the fallen spirits and He went there to rescue His own who were there waiting for Him. In Ephesians 4:7 we read, "Therefore it says, 'When He ascended on high, He led captive a host of captives, and He gave gifts to men.' " Now this expression, 'He ascended,' what does it mean except that He also had descended into the lower parts of the earth? And the answer to the question does not make any sense, unless He descended into the lower parts of the earth. What does it mean, "He led a host of captives, captive"? The Old Testament believers were captive, even though they were not suffering. But they were captive and they were a host. When Christ ascended from hell, this host of captives was led captive with Christ. I do not see how we can combine Ephesians 4 with I Peter 3 unless we come to that conclusion.

In conclusion then, we will see that Jesus Christ did not descend to suffer. He went to proclaim judgment to the unbelieving spirits and He went to preach vindication to those who had died in the faith. Every man has one of two captors. You will either spend eternity in the clutches of Christ or in the clutches of death. It has to be one or the other. And what I believe that we can glean from the teaching that Christ descended into hell, is that He descended there to teach us that He is ever ready, by His blood that has been shed, to vindicate the believer. If we only had a gospel which included only New Testament believers, and the Old Testament believers were somehow left up in the air, I would be very insecure with that. God's Word is true. Christ will not lose one sheep. If you will come to Him, He will vindicate your faith in Him forever. "My sheep hear My voice, and I know them, and they follow Me; and I give eternal life to them, and they shall never perish; and no one is able to snatch them out of the Father's hand." (John 10:27, 28)

"THE THIRD DAY HE ROSE AGAIN FROM THE DEAD"
Romans 4:24, 25

There is a story of a man who owns a field and rents it to Mr. Jones for $100. When the time comes for the payment, Mr. Jones says, "I'm awfully sorry, it's been a bad season, it was too dry at the wrong time, it was too wet at the wrong time, I just don't have the $100 to pay you. But if you will take half of my crop and be satisfied with that, I'd be pleased." No matter what Mr. Jones wants to do, it is up to the owner of the field, whether or not the debt will be cleared. If the owner wishes to say, "All right Mr. Jones, I'll take one half of the crop and we'll call that an end to the debt," that settles the matter. If he says, "I'll take 25% of the crop and call it a settlement of the debt," that is the end of the matter. And if he should say, "Mr. Jones, if you will just sing me a beautiful love song, I'll call that the end of the debt," that will settle the matter. The point is that the owner is able to jutify the debtor because the owner has that privilege. That story illustrates the truth of the text that we come to in this portion of the Apostles' Creed. It is the connection of the resurrection of Jesus Christ to our justification that will occupy our attention here.

Let us examine, first of all, the meaning of justification.

Second, man's attempts to justify himself. Third, the fact that God is the Justifier of men by Christ. In Romans 4:24, 25 we read, "But for our sake, also, to whom it will be reckoned, as those who believe in Him who raised Jesus our Lord from the dead, He who was delivered up because of our transgressions, and was raised because of our justification."

The last phrase is the most important. If you understand what the phrase teaches, you will understand clearly what it means to be justified by God, by the resurrection. It is "raised *because* of our justification," not for our justification. Justification is the judicial act of God whereby the believing elect are washed forever from all guilt. That is what it means to be justified. The one that God uses to justify us is Christ. Somewhere in God's heaven the gavel falls, clearing every believer of debt to God. Justification, then, is an objective change in our relationship to God's Law. It is the legal side to our salvation. We read in Job 9:20, 21, "Though I am righteous, my mouth will condemn me; though I am guiltless, He will declare me guilty. I am guiltless; I do not take notice of myself; I despise my life." So justification is not an experimental change in the life of the Christian, but it is a judicial act carried out by God on our behalf. Now, look at Romans 5:9. "Much more then, having now been justified by His blood, we shall be saved from the wrath of God through Him." Now look at Romans 5:1. "Therefore having been justified by faith." "Which is it?", you say. "Are we justified by faith, or are we justified by blood?" By faith, yes; by blood, yes; by other things, yes; even the resurrection. But the important thing to see here is that God is the Justifier, regardless of the means which He uses to do that. One of the best ways to define something is to be able to state what it is not, and that is where we can look at this point now for the difference between justification, sanctification, redemption and forgiveness.

REGENERATION

First, justification is not regeneration. What is regeneration? What is generation? We often talk about electrical generators which you crank it up to get a light. Regeneration is putting life back into that which was dead. So when God comes into a man's life by His Holy Spirit and calls him to faith we can

70

equate regeneration with what you and I call the new birth or being born again. Look at Romans 8:30. "And whom He predestined, these He also called; and whom He called, these He also justified; and whom He justified, these He also glorified." So regeneration is an act of God's Spirit upon your life, whereas justification is the sentence of God the Judge, having declared that you are free from all guilt. Furthermore, regeneration makes room for me in God's family, but justification gives me a place to stand before His judgment throne. I use the word "stand" as against "fall". Regeneration makes me a part of God's family. Justification makes me be able to withstand the judgment, because it has already fallen upon Christ.

SANCTIFICATION

Second, justification is not only not regeneration, but justification is not sanctification either. Sanctification is what God does in me by the Holy Spirit. Justification is what God has done for me by Christ. Sanctification brings us into an ever-increasing awareness of the gap that is naturally between God Almighty and us sinners. Sanctification is that process by which the Holy Spirit brings us into deeper knowledge of the Word, deeper knowledge of our sin, deeper knowledge of the fact that we never really deserved to be saved in the first place. Sanctification is not perfectionism. We do not get better and better throughout the Christian life. We do not necessarily sin less and less, but what we become aware of more and more is that our sin grieves God. So sanctification is that which the Spirit does in us. Justification is that which God has done for us by Christ.

FORGIVENESS

Third, justification is not only regeneration, it is not sanctification, it is not forgiveness either. Do not confuse justification with forgiveness. They are similar only in that God performs all of them. God is our Justifier and God is also the One who procures our forgiveness, but they are not the same thing. Forgiveness concerns my deeds; justification concerns me. There is a distinction between those two. God justifies me according to my belief in the Lord Jesus Christ's atonement for me. But God forgives me for *my sins.*

71

We need to see what man's attempts are to justify himself. Let us return to the opening illustration. Mr. Jones cannot say to the owner of the field, "Look, all I have is a 30% crop and you are going to have to take that, that is all I have." That is the way the world looks at God. "Lord, you want me? You will have to take me the way I am." God never takes us the way we are. He comes to us in our depravity, but receives us as Christ's own purchased property. God does not draw us to Himself as a sinner who have no ransom paid, but as Christ's brethren. Religion is the first thing that man uses to justify himself. Romans 1:18 says, "For even though they (the natural man) knew God, they did not honor Him as God, or give thanks; but they became futile in their speculations, and their foolish heart was darkened. Professing to be wise, they became fools, and exchanged the glory of the incorruptible God for an image in the form of corruptible man and of birds and four-footed animals and crawling creatures." So whether he is dealing with a religious superstition based upon a totem pole, or upon an image of stone, or an image of wood, man in his natural state tries to justify himself according to his religion. It is true that man is a religious being. Being created by God how could he not be a religious being? But as Isaiah sarcastically points out in part of his prophecy, a man will take a piece of wood, burn half of it, watch it go up in smoke and then worship the other half. And in his depravity, and in his foolishness, he expects God will be appeased by his religiosity. But that is not the way it works. In effect God says, "If you approach Me in any other way but by My Son, there is no way you can be justified, there is no way the debt can be cancelled, there is no way you can stand before My throne cleared." Your best is not good enough aside from Jesus Christ.

Now will you turn to John 10:14-18. "I am the good shepherd; and I know My own, and My own know Me, even as the Father knows Me and I know the Father; and I lay down My life for the sheep. And I have other sheep, which are not of this fold (speaking of the Gentiles) I must bring them also, and they shall hear My voice; and they shall become one flock with one shepherd. For this reason the Father Loves Me, because I lay down My life that I may take it again. (There is the first reference to the resurrection). No one has taken it away from

Me, but I lay it down on My own initiative. I have authority to lay it down, and I have authority to take it up again. This commandment I received from My Father."

We are never going to understand Christianity if we do not understand that God the Father delivered up God the Son to be killed. That is crucial to our theology. God delivered up Christ to die for us. It was not a mistake and Christ did not just feel like dying. God ordained the death of His Son as "the Lamb slain from before the foundation of the world." Caiphas was part of the trial, but that does not matter. Pilate was part of the trial, but that does not matter. That is all secondary. What is primary is that you see God delivering His Son to the cross for us. If it were any other way, God could not be the Justifier of those who believe in Christ. Peter preached this in Acts 2:22, 23. "Men of Israel, listen to these words: Jesus the Nazarene, a man attested to you by God with miracles and wonders and signs which God performed through Him in your midst, just as you yourselves know — this Man, delivered up by the predetermined plan and foreknowledge of God, you nailed to a cross by the hands of godless men and put Him to death." How clear that is! We will fail to understand the basic foundation of biblical theology if we fail to see that God delivered Christ to be killed.

What then is justification? It is not regeneration; it is not sanctification; it is not forgiveness. It is the act whereby God, once and for all, clears the guilt from His believing elect.

We also have to know the agent by which He justifies us, and that is Christ. Christ has died for us; we have to know Him in order to know the Father who delivered Christ to us. What else could Jesus mean in John 14:6 when He says, "I am the way, and the truth, and the life; no one comes to the Father, but through Me." No man can know the Justifier until he first knows the Savior. It is the *resurrection* that guarantees the justification of the saints, not the atonement. The atonement does not guarantee the justification; it is the resurrection that does that. The doctrines of the atonement and justification both stem from God's grace and both are indispensable to our salvation.

What does justification mean? That God, once for all, clears His people from their guilt. How can He do that? Because His perfect Son, who never sinned, died on the cross, and you never have to show up for your deserved execution. That is what makes it possible for Him to justify us. Now that is how the atonement is related to our justification. But let us see how the resurrection is related to our justification. Were Jesus Christ still dead today, we would have absolutely no assurance that we were justified. The debt has been paid, but how do we know that God was satisfied with that? We know that God was satisfied with it by raising Him from the dead. God raised Christ to prove to us that we are justified and that there will never be another sacrifice because God is fully satisfied with the death of His own Son. Let me give you an illustration. As long as the security is locked up or is imprisoned, the debt cannot be paid. As long as Christ were to remain dead, my debt is not paid, not cleared. God raised Christ as a result of the justification. Christ was not raised from the dead in order to justify us, but He was raised because God had already justified us. If the debt has been paid and the receipt is in our hand, who can charge us again?

Has the gavel of God's justification fallen for you? If you do not know, I invite you to search the Scriptures. "Be diligent to present yourself approved to God as a workman who does not need to be ashamed, handling accurately the word of truth." (II Timothy 2:15)

"HE ASCENDED INTO HEAVEN, AND SITTETH ON THE RIGHT HAND OF GOD THE FATHER ALMIGHTY"

Hebrews 10:11, 12

What does the word "Bethlehem" bring to your mind? I trust that it will be the incarnation of Christ. What does the word "Calvary" bring to your mind? I would think that the cross of Christ and His work as the Lamb of God being slain for His people would come to mind. If I were to say "Concord Bridge" or "Boston Tea Party" I would trust that the early steps of the American Revolution would come to your mind. Similarly, the word "Ascension" should speak of Christ's office as our High Priest. "And every priest stands daily ministering and offering time after time the same sacrifices, which can never take away sins; but He, having offered one sacrifice for sins for all time, sat down at the right hand of God." (Hebrews 10:11, 12) We shall deal briefly with the Ascension and at length with Christ as our High Priest.

Dealing with the Ascension first, turn to Acts 1 and see what the opening verses say about the Ascension of our Lord Jesus Christ. It is important to know that He did ascend into heaven because His seating at the right hand of the Father follows it. In verse 9 of Acts 1 we read: "And after He had said these things, He was lifted up while they were looking on, and a cloud received Him out of their sight." This is the record of the Ascension of Christ to His office as High Priest at the right hand of the Father.

Christ's office as prophet has ceased. Jesus Christ is no longer teaching as a prophet except by His Spirit through the Word, of course. Furthermore, His office as High Priest really commenced even before the Ascension. Satan had demanded permission of God to sift Peter like wheat, but Christ said "I have prayed for you and it will not happen". That means that He already had interceded for Peter and so the office of His High Priesthood interceding between us and the Father really was already operative before the Ascension. We believe He ascended, but why He ascended is more important and should consume more of our time. Christ's office as our High Priest is connected with the sacrificial economy of the Old Testament, particularly as it is described in Leviticus 16. Nowhere in Scripture does God explain His disgust at the misinterpretation of the Old Testament sacrificial system than you find in Isaiah 1. It is a scathing rebuke to anyone who would dare try to approach God on a spiritual plane, kidding themselves to think that they actually could approach Him with the sacrifice of animals. "Hear the word of the Lord, you rulers of Sodom; give ear to the instruction of our God, you people of Gomorrah. 'What are your multiplied sacrifices to Me?' says the Lord. 'I have had enough of burnt offerings of rams, and the fat of fed cattle. And I take no pleasure in the blood of bulls, lambs, or goats. When you come to appear before Me, who requires of you this trampling of My courts? Bring your worthless offerings no longer, their incense is an abomination to Me. New moon and sabbath, the calling of assemblies — I cannot endure inequity and the solemn assembly. I hate your new moon festivals and your appointed feasts, they have become a burden to Me. I am weary of bearing them. So when you spread out your hands in prayer, I will hide My eyes from you, yes, even though you multiply your prayers, I will not listen. Your hands are full of bloodshed.' " (Isaiah 1:10-15) Now how could you possibly think after reading those verses that God is somehow interested in sacrificing animals? Along with everything else in the Scriptures, man has found many ways to pervert sound doctrine. We read in Ecclesiastes 7:29 that "God made man upright but man has sought out many devices." You give man anything that is pure and he will corrupt it as soon as he touches it. Give him an idea from Scripture, a doctrine from Scripture, and it will become perverse and false as soon as he begins to speak it. It is man's nature to pollute that which is pure. Now that is not the only place in Scripture that we find it. We know from this passage that never in God's eyes were the sacrifices of animals to be effectual for the covering of man's sins. It was only a prefiguration of the Lamb of God who would come. In other words, the sacrifice of animals in the Old Testament no more forgave the sins of the people who lived in the Old Testament time than does your participation in the Lord's Supper forgive your sins. Christ's death is what has forgiven us, not the Lord's Supper. It is Christ's death that forgave Abraham, not the sacrifice of animals. Both were given as an aid to the righteous that they might understand the doctrine of the atonement of Christ. Now, look back at Leviticus 16:7-10 where we get the early description of the blood sacrifice of animals and how we are to understand what Jesus Christ was going to do Himself? " 'And he shall take the two goats and present them before the Lord at the doorway of the tent of meeting. And Aaron shall cast lots for the two goats, one lot for the Lord and the other lot for the scapegoat. Then Aaron shall offer the goat on which the lot for the Lord fell, and make it a sin offering. (In other words, kill it.) But the goat on which the lot for the scapegoat fell, shall be presented alive before the Lord, to make atonement upon it, to send it into the wilderness as the scapegoat.' " Now here is the teaching of those few verses fulfilled in the Lord Jesus Christ. A first goat was killed. The blood of that goat was drained into a bowl and the priest would have taken that to the tabernacle all the way up to the Holy of Holies and would have sprinkled it upon the mercy seat. Some of that blood would have been poured upon the head of the second goat. That goat was not killed, but was sent out into the wilderness. Now the blood taken into the mercy seat did not for one minute atone for the sins of the people and not for one minute did the goat that was sent into the wilderness actually remove the sin and the guilt of Israel from them. But God was using these means to teach Israel what the Lamb of God would do when He came. And Christ did those two things in Himself. He presented Himself as a living sacrifice to God. He Himself was the altar, the priest, and the victim all in one, and on the other hand, the blood of Christ has also removed our sins from us as far as east is from west. So, we find it in Isaiah I that God never says that the shedding of animal blood is effectual to the covering of man's sin. Back in Leviticus we see the teaching of the two goats, pointing to what Christ would do when He came. Spurgeon said the doctrines of the Gospel are like the quarters of the universe as seen through an astronomer's telescope. What he meant by that is that you cannot take the doctrines of the New Testament and squeeze them down to one little shaft of meaning. But when you look through the resurrection of Christ and view all of Scripture through His death and resurrection, then the panorama of Scriptural doctrine in its entirety opens up as it was revealed to be. Look at Hebrews 10:11a. "And every priest stands daily." Let us just stop there. The word "daily" is important and the word "stand" is important. I need to say something about Old Testament priests. In general, they were a corrupt bunch. We read a very clear-cut story about them in I Samuel 2:12-17. "Now the sons of Eli were worthless men; they did not know the Lord and the custom of the priests with the people. When any man was offering a sacrifice, the priest's servant would come while the meat was boiling, with a three-pronged fork in his hand. Then he would thrust it into the pan, or kettle, or caldron, or pot; all that the fork brought up the priest would take for himself. Thus they did in Shiloh to all the Israelites who came there. Also, before they burned the fat, the priest's servant would come and say to the man who was sacrificing, 'Give the priest meat for roasting, as he will not take boiled meat from you, only raw.' And if the man said to him, 'They must surely burn the fat first, and then take as much as you desire,' then he would say, 'No, but you shall give it to me now; and if not, I will take it by force.' Thus the sin of the young men was very great before the Lord, for the men despised the offering of the Lord." And to cap it off, drop your eyes down to verse 22. "Now Eli was very old; and he heard all that his sons were doing to all Israel, and how they lay with the women who served at the doorway of the tent of meeting." In other words, during the priests' "off-hours" they were fornicating with the women who were lying about at the tent of meeting.

78

These were despicable people. Wherever a human priesthood has been established, its ends and means of existence have been corrupt. Why? Because there is no priestly intercession between God and man except Jesus Christ. (I Timothy 2:5) Men need a reliable, perpetual, sinless priest.

Now note the latter part of verse 11. "And every priest stands daily." The word "stand" is important because it implies that work is not yet done. Note how that contrasts to Jesus Christ sitting at the right hand of the Father. Why is He sitting? Because His work as sacrifice is done. It is over, complete, and He is not going to die again. There is not going to be another sacrifice. Someone may ask, "Why does Stephen say he saw Jesus Christ standing at the right hand of the Father, not sitting?" There Stephen sees a risen Christ standing and waiting to receive him into heaven. But the fact that Hebrews records that He is seated at the right hand of the Father is to teach us that the work of the Atonement is completed. That perpetual shedding of blood is all over with and it is a marvelous truth for all of us who believe in Christ. We know that God will never again require of us a sacrifice of blood — our blood! Christ is it.

Now look at verse 12. "But He, having offered one sacrifice for sins for all time,, sat down at the right hand of God." This verse and verse 10 of this chapter are verses which proved beyond any shadow of a doubt that the "mass" is unbiblical and is anti-Christ in its performance. What are the results of the offering of Jesus Christ, Himself, He being the priest, the victim and the offering all at once? Well, the first result was that He sits at the right hand of the Father. The second result was that sitting at the right hand of the Father His work is now complete for you and me to understand it as such. Turn to I John 2:1. "My little children, I am writing these things to you that you may not sin. And if anyone sins, we have an Advocate with the Father, Jesus Christ the righteous." That is a great verse. Why is it a great verse? Because we continue to sin. An advocate is a Paraclete. A Paraclete is one that comes to your side when you need aid. This answers the questions that many Romanists ask. "Are only the sins that we ask forgiveness for, forgiven?" If it were that way, certainly we would all end up in hell. For those sins that we either forget that we have committed or are ignorant of, even the ones in which we persist, the Spirit constantly intercedes for us. "And in the same way the Spirit also helps our weakness; for we do not know how to pray as we should, but the Spirit Himself intercedes for us with groanings too deep for words." (Romans 8:26) Do not glean from that teaching, "Oh, I can do what I want." I have yet to meet a true Christian who is practicing sin because he knows that he has a scapegoat in Christ. That is not the way the Spirit leads us. We also see from I John 2:1 that it is possible not to sin. I do not mean by that it is possible to abstain from sinning from the time you are re-born onward. But obviously it is possible to live periods of your life, whether they be minutes long or even hours long, without sinning or else the verse would not be there. "I am writing these things to you that you may not sin. And if anyone sins, we have an Advocate with the Father, Jesus Christ the righteous."

Now when we are talking about advocates and Paracletes and lawyers, we need to understand what "pleading" means in the Scriptures. Jesus Christ pleads *with* the Father *for* us. Christ does not plead with the unbeliever to receive Him. It is very important to see that distinction. The Spirit of Christ regenerates us with a power that we are not even able to control. First, our sense of moral obligation begins to change and our sense of what human depravity is becomes enlightened, and we are led step by step by the Spirit to a knowledge of Christ. But Christ never pleads with us. He pleads with the Father for us. So what happens if we commit murder? We have an Advocate. What happens if we commit adultery? We have an Advocate. What happens if we cheat? We have an Advocate. What happens if we lie? We have an Advocate. What if we gossip? We have an Advocate.

Yet, I John 2:1 shows us that we are to refrain from sin. We belong to Christ. God has called us to be holy and blameless. How can we mirror Christ if when someone looks into the mirror of our lives he sees nothing but a big, black smudge? We have seen that Christ has redeemed us by His blood; we have seen that we have been justified by His blood and .by our faith in Him, which God has given us as a gift, and because God raised Him from the dead as a receipt to show us that He will never again present us with the bill of our need to be justified. He raised Christ and He is not going to demand any more sacrifices. Now we see that Jesus Christ has ascended and He is sitting at the right hand of the Father as our Intercessor.

Why? Because we still sin. Christ's work as our High Priest is what makes the truth of Romans 8:31-39 so applicable and reassuring. "What then shall we say to these things? If God is for us, who is against us? He who did not spare His own Son, but delivered Him up for us all, how will He not also with Him freely give us all things? Who will bring a charge against God's elect? God is the one who justifies; who is the one who condemns? Christ Jesus is He who died, yes, rather who was raised, who is at the right hand of God, who also intercedes for us. Who shall separate us from the love of Christ? Shall tribulation, or distress, or persecution, or famine, or nakedness, or peril, or sword? Just as it is written, 'For Thy sake we are being put to death all day long; we were considered as sheep to be slaughtered.' But in all these things we overwhelmingly conquer through Him who loved us. For I am convinced that neither death, nor life, nor angels, nor principalities, nor things present, nor things to come, nor powers, nor height, nor depth, nor any other created thing, shall be able to separate us from the love of God, which is in Christ Jesus our Lord."

"FROM THENCE HE SHALL COME TO JUDGE THE QUICK AND THE DEAD"
II Timothy 4:1

It is time to say that the sins of all men must be judged. There are two days which are yet to take place in world history, both of which are extremely important for us to understand concerning biblical judgment. One is the Day of the Lord and the other is the Day of Jesus Christ. The former is the day of judgment, the latter the day of union between Christ and His people.

The Day of the Lord is a day of judgment upon both the Gentiles and Israel. The hearts and the deeds of men will be examined for what they are: fallen and unrighteous in God's eyes. It is terrifying indeed for those who are not covered by the blood of Christ. In Isaiah 2:12 we read: "For the Lord of hosts will have a day of reckoning against everyone who is proud and lofty, and against everyone who is lifted up, that he may be abased." Then in Isaiah 13:6, 9, 10, "Wail, for the day of the Lord is near! It will come as destruction from the Almighty. Behold, the day of the Lord is coming, cruel, with fury and burning anger, to make the land a desolation; and He will exterminate its sinners from it. For the stars of heaven and their constellations will not flash forth their light, the sun will be dark when it rises, and the moon will not shed its light." Then in Amos 5:18-20 we read, "Alas, you who are longing for the day of the Lord, for what purpose will the day of the Lord be to you? It will be darkness and not light; as when a man flees from a lion, and a bear meets him, or goes home, leans his hand against the wall, and a snake bites him. Will not the day of the Lord be darkness instead of light, even gloom with no brightness in it?"

Then in the New Testament we read in II Peter 3:10, "But the day of the Lord will come like a thief, in which the heavens will pass away with a roar and the elements will be destroyed with intense heat, and the earth and its works will be burned up." This is the Day of the Lord! It has not yet come. It is going to come and it is going to be furious and terrible. Those who face this judgment will not be able to defend themselves against it in any way.

The Day of the Lord is different from the Day of Christ. The Day of Christ is a happy day. That is the Day that we read about in I Thessalonians 4:16, 17. "For the Lord Himself will descend from heaven with a shout, with the voice of the archangel, and with the trumpet of God; and the dead in Christ shall rise first. Then we who are alive and remain shall be caught up together with them in the clouds to meet the Lord in the air, and thus we shall always be with the Lord." But the Day of the Lord is a day of judgment against the nonbeliever in which no believer will participate. Very briefly, the chronology is as follows: The Day of Christ takes place. Then the tribulation is to follow. Then comes the great and terrible Day of the Lord, which is the culmination of all the world history where everyone from the beast to Satan, the false prophet, and all unbelievers are to be judged according to their works and cast into the lake of fire.

Now, let us look at the judgment of those who reject Christ. Men are not necessarily condemned because they reject the Gospel. You can be condemned without rejecting the Gospel. You can be condemned as Romans 1 says, simply because you do not live up to the light of God's revelation which He has stamped on your very image and upon the nature in which we live. Romans 1:18 says, "For the wrath of God is revealed from heaven against all ungodliness and unrighteousness of men, who suppress the truth in unrighteousness." Note first of all that to suppress truth does not mean to destroy truth. Man suppresses the truth that God exists, but they are not able to destroy that evidence. That is the first reason in the next three verses which calls man to be accountable for his knowledge of God even though he refuses to honor Him.

In verse 19, the reason is given why he is not held without excuse. "Because that which is known about God is evident within them; for God made it evident to them." How did God make it evident? "For since the creation of the world His invisible attributes, His eternal power and divine nature, have been clearly seen, being understood through what has been made, so that they are without excuse." Note two words in that verse: "invisibile" in the first sentence and "clearly" in the second. "His invisible attributes have been clearly seen." That is paradoxical. Verse 21 is the key. "For even though they knew God, (note that they did know Him and there are no atheists, truly speaking) they did not honor Him as God, or give thanks; but they became futile in their speculations, and their foolish heart was darkened. Professing to be wise, they became fools, and exchanged the glory of the incorruptible God for an image in the form of corruptible man and of birds and four-footed animals and crawling creatures." Men stand judged before God because they will not honor the God that they know to exist. There are no true atheists. We will not win anyone to Christ by reason. Our job is to speak the words of the Gospel and it is the Holy Spirit's work to apply that to the heart of the nonbeliever.

Now someone will say, "How do we know that men are condemned on this basis and this basis alone?" The Gospel of Christ was not introduced into the world to judge the unbelievers. It was introduced as the means by which God was going to call to Himself the elect. It was a positive move, not a negative one. Men are judged apart from the Gospel. We read about it very clearly in John 3:17-19. "For God did not send the Son into the world to judge the world; but that the world should be saved through Him. He who believes in Him is not judged; he who does not believe has been judged already, because he has not believed in the name of the only begotten Son of God. And this is the judgment, that the light is come into the world, and men loved the darkness rather than the light; for their deeds were evil."

Men are judged already. They do not need to reject Christ to be condemned. They are sinners by birth, sinners by choice, and sinners by enjoyment, and therefore, are judged for the same. We all are examples of Romans 1:18-21 were it not for Christ's intervention in our lives. That is the way by which we are able to understand our salvation in Him. We cannot get to God through the creation. Jesus said, "I am the way, the truth and the life, no man comes to the Father but through Me."

God's judgment upon the nations is also something that must be studied when we talk about judgment. Psalm 2 gives us a view of a conversation involving all three members of the Trinity and the rulers of the earth. Dr. Donald G. Barnhouse, in his book *The Invisible War*, phrased it this way:

"The Holy Spirit (with sorrow). 'Why do the nations rage, and the people imagine a vain thing? The kings of the earth set themselves and the rulers take counsel together, against the Lord, and against his anointed.

"The Kings (with bravado). 'Let us break their bands asunder, and cast away their cords from us!

"The Holy Spirit (with scorn). 'He that sitteth in the heavens shall laugh; the Lord shall have them in derision. Then shall he speak unto them in his wrath, and terrify them in his sore displeasure.'

"God the Father (with majesty). 'Yet I have set my king upon my holy hill of Zion.'

"Jesus Christ (unfolding a scroll and reading). 'I will declare the decree: the Lord hath said unto me,

Thou art my Son, this day have I begotten thee. Ask of me, and I shall give thee the nations for thine inheritance, and the uttermost parts of the earth for thy possession.'

"God the Father (with joy). 'Thou shalt break them with a rod of iron; thou shalt dash them in pieces like a potter's vessel.'

"The Holy Spirit (with pleading). 'Be wise now, therefore, O ye kings; be instructed O ye judges of the earth. Serve the Lord with fear, and rejoice with trembling. Embrace the Son, lest he be angry, and ye perish from the way, when his wrath is kindled but a little. Blessed are all they that put their trust in him.' "

Now let us turn explicitly to the judgment of the great white throne, which we find in Revelation 20. What is most enlightening about this particular chapter of Revelation is that we really get the only clear window in Scriptures to see just how the judgment will take place and on what basis God will reward the righteous and will condemn the unrighteous. Revelation 20:11-15 reads: "And I saw a great white throne and Him who sat upon it, from whose presence earth and heaven fled away, and no place was found for them. And I saw the dead, the great and the small, standing before the throne, and the books were opened; and another book was opened, which is the book of life; and the dead were judged from the things which were written in the books, according to their deeds. And the sea gave up the dead which were in it, and death and Hades gave up the dead which were in them; and they were judged, every one of them according to their deeds. And death and Hades were thrown into the lake of fire. This is the second death, the lake of fire. And if anyone's name was not found written in the book of life, he was thrown into the lake of fire."

Christ, at this great and terrible day of the Lord, is sitting upon the throne. The dead are standing before the throne. The Day of Christ has long since taken place and the raptured saints are with Christ. Look clearly at verse 12. See the difference between books (plural) and book (singular). There is only one Lamb's Book of Life. In that Book is written the names of God's elect, every one of His chosen ones who shall not be snatched out of the hand of the Redeemer, each one for whom Christ has died. Anyone whose name is not found in that Book is cast into the Lake of Fire. But how are those who are to be condemned judged? On what basis? It says, "According to their deeds." Now, if we were all judged according to our deeds, we would all go to hell. The reason that the believer is not judged according to his deeds, is that he has already been judged according to the death of Christ who has died for him.

Now, if you will picture in your mind a rectangle, let us divide the rectangle in half. The space above the line is heaven and the space below the line is hell. It does not matter if you are one inch above the line or five inches. Heaven is heaven. It does not matter if you are an inch below the line, or two feet below the line; hell is hell. Those whose names are not found in the Lamb's Book of Life find themselves in this lower category. They are judged, but they will be judged according to their deeds. In other words, some men will not only be in hell, but will further be judged according to their deeds. Judas-Iscariot and Esau are both in hell but probably are at different levels of judgment. The righteous are all in heaven, but are rewarded according to their good works in God's Name. Something here is very important. God forgets all of the evil deeds of His believers because of Christ. He only rewards us. But no matter how many good deeds the non-believers have done, those deeds do not count. They are judged only according to their evil deeds. So the righteous have the evil deeds blotted out, and the unrighteous have all of their "so-called" good deeds blotted out. There is an eternal separation between the two and God will reward the righteous and He will judge the wicked.

All evil and rebelliousness of man's heart is going to be exposed at this judgment. But no one who comes to Christ has any need to ever see that day. No one who comes to Christ ever needs to stand before the great white throne. God's wrath is a consuming fire. It cannot be stopped. It is ordained, it will take place, and it will be just as severe as it says it will be. I can remember talking with many people throughout the Viet Nam conflict about the cruelty of man to man. And stories began to emerge from various sources of the "tiger cages" and the other torture instruments that were used upon prisoners of war in Viet Nam. But even in the height of man's cruelty to his fellow man, there is still a point in man's nature where he breaks down himself and is willing to relinquish, or to back off from the judgment he has cast upon someone else. But God cannot do that. Once He has consigned you to hell, that is the end. He does not say, "All right, you have served your time." He does not feel sorry for you after 10,000 years. It is closed and final. Why? Because He is holy and we are unholy, and He has prescribed only one way by which we can come to Him: by

Christ. If you are not a believer in the Lord Jesus Christ, the dam of God's wrath is going to break upon you because it already has fallen on Christ for the believer, and if you will have none of Christ, God will have none of you.

God is the One who clears us; Christ is the one who pays the debt. He is the substitute. But you cannot know the Father without knowing the Substitute. You are certainly not going to know either one of them if you do not come to Him. God is not a liar. I have yet to meet anyone who has said to me, "I came to Christ and He cast me out." No one will ever say it to me because I know God is not a liar.

"I BELIEVE IN THE HOLY GHOST"
John 14:26

In this Creed, the salvific work of each member of the Trinity is clearly seen. It is true to say that each member of the Trinity has an integral part in our salvation. A very cursory view of our salvation and probably one that most Christians have is that Jesus Christ is our Savior and that is the end of the matter. If you dig into the Scriptures, you will find the reason Jesus Christ came to earth was to die for certain people that God had elected to salvation. Yet, even with the elective mark of the Father and the redemptive mark of the Son, man still cannot comprehend any of that without the Holy Spirit applying it to his heart. This is what will hold our attention at this point. John 14:26 is our text of departure. "But the Helper, the Holy Spirit, whom the Father will send in My name, He will teach you all things, and bring to your remembrance all that I said to you." That verse tells us two things. First, it is the Spirit that does the teaching, not the preacher. Second, if you are being taught by God's Spirit, He will teach you of Christ and what He says. The Holy Spirit generates us, adopts us and sanctifies us. But we are going to focus this evening upon His regenerative work in our hearts.

That regenerative work which He does is done in the heart of a man long before the man becomes aware of the fact that the Spirit is even there. In other words, conception and fertilization must preceed the new birth. One of the first things the Spirit does is to constrain a man's moral conscience long before he will admit that there is a God or a Christ. The Spirit leads that man to the point where he understands eventually what the biblical revelation is of his salvation in Christ. So when I talk of the regenerative work of the Holy Spirit, I am talking about one and the same of four things. The new birth, conversion, what it means to be a new creation in Christ, and spiritually, the resurrection of the dead. All four of those things mean the regeneration of the individual by the Holy Spirit. The Holy Spirit's work of regeneration is that taking of a depraved human being and transforming that individual into a holy, acceptable individual before God. God's elect are called to faith at different times. The Holy Spirit applies the redemption of Christ to the individual.

Let us look further at this application. I have said that the Holy Spirit, in His first step of regenerating us does a work of application. He applies to our understanding the meaning of Christ's redemption. Let me illustrate. I can remember being severely burned by hot water. We were in England in 1968 visiting with a Liverpool surgeon. He gave us instruction about the house before we went there. He said, "Be careful, the water that comes out of the hot water tap is 211°, just one degree below boiling." Well, I did a foolish thing. I was drawing myself a bath and I turned on the hot water first, which is what I usually do in my own home, and out it came at 211°. I had a plastic cup in my hand that I was going to use to catch some water and rinse out the tub. It burned my finger so badly that I flicked the cup out of my hand and sprayed this boiling water all over my chest. I was in agony and in no time I had big red blotches surface. Fortunately, my wife had packed an ointment for burns and which relieved the pain.

Now let us look at that situation a little more clearly. Here was the problem: I had been scalded. The remedy for that problem was the ointment. But that ointment had to be applied to the burn if there was going to be any healing. So here is a man who is depraved, who does not know God, who, Paul says, is the natural man. Here is Christ, who has died for God's people. The remedy is perfect, it cannot be any better, and the man cannot be any more depraved. But until the Holy Spirit takes this truth and applies it to the heart of that unbeliever, nothing is going to happen in that life. But as soon as the Holy Spirit drives the application of the redemption of Christ to the heart, you have what is called the new birth. One way, then, to view this is its connection to election. The fact that the Holy Spirit is working in an individual and beginning to bring him to a knowledge of Christ presupposes God's election of that individual. In other words, another way to look at election is that God's elect are those in whom the Spirit is applying the doctrine of redemption. God chooses us, Christ dies for us, but we do not know this until the Holy Spirit applies that to us and indwells us.

Someone will say, "If the natural man despises the Spirit of God, (which he does) then how does the Spirit of God bring that despising heart to a point where it loves God, instead of despising Him?" Well, it might seem like a difficult question to answer, but it is quite simple. It is like asking, "How is a dirty car going to get clean?" That is simple — you wash it. Well, a heart that despises God is not going to love God on its own. It has to be transformed. That is one of the manifestations of God's Spirit applying to our hearts the redemption of Jesus Christ. I believe we can get closer to this truth by looking at Adam. Adam was neither a beast nor what theologians call a pneumatic (spirit). Adam was a combination of a beast and a pneumatic. He was a human being who had a soul. God says He breathed into Adam the breath of life. When Adam fell into disobedience, that disrupted his relationship to God. The spiritual fall left Adam only one feeble directing guide and that is what we call our conscience. And a conscience is a very untrustworthy instrument because it gleans its standards from human standards. You see, the most perverse man in the world has a conscience. And what you and I would call a moral man has a conscience. There are certain things that are right and wrong for him. But whether it is a human moral standard or whether it is an inhumane depraved standard, neither of them come anywhere near God's standard of righteousness. So we need more than a conscience, we need God's indwelling spirit to lead us into the truth of Christ without which we will never know anything about God. Man cannot subject himself naturally to God's law. Further, a man cannot even say, "Jesus Christ is Lord" except the Holy Spirit lead him to say that.

Again, I Corinthians 2:14, the natural man does not understand the things of the Spirit. Why? Because they are spiritually discerned and the truth of Christ has not been applied to the natural man. Paul says, the natural man does not perceive the things of the Spirit until the Holy Spirit applies the redemption of Christ to him. As soon as that happens, then the natural man becomes a super-natural man, or a spiritual man, and does understand the things of the spirit. That is why you can preach the Gospel a hundred times to a man and he still stands there dumbfounded, confused, baffled and does not comprehend it. It is not because there is something wrong with the preacher; it is not because there is something wrong with the humidity in the room; it is because the natural man does not perceive the things of the Spirit. And until the Spirit applies the knowledge of Christ to his heart, he will never understand.

Now turn to John 3. The conversation that Jesus has with Nicodemus best describes to us the work of the Holy Spirit in a man's heart. Nicodemus does not understand anything, but he is searching. Why is he searching? Well, I believe that the Holy Spirit was at work in Nicodemus' heart long before he came to Christ that night. From what we understand of the post-crucifixion portions of the Gospels, Nicodemus was there to help Joseph of Arimathea bury Christ. I believe Nicodemus came to faith. I believe that he was a believer and I believe that he became one of the disciples in Jerusalem. In John 3:3-8 we read: "Jesus answered and said to him, 'Truly, truly, I say to you, unless one is born again, he cannot see the kingdom of God.' Nicodemus said to Him, 'How can a man be born when he is old? He cannot enter a second time into his mother's womb and be born, can he?' Jesus answered, 'Truly, truly, I say to you, unless one is born of water and the Spirit, he cannot enter the kingdom of God. That which is born of the flesh is flesh; and that which is born of the Spirit is spirit. Do not marvel that I said to you, 'You must be born again.' (Now here is the key.) The wind blows where it wishes and you hear the sound of it, but do not know where it comes from and where it is going; so is every one who is born of the Spirit.' "

To be born again, then, means to be born of the Spirit of God, which means to be regenerate. When Jesus says here that you must be born of water and the Spirit, His reference to water here does not refer to baptism. There are three reasons why it does not. First of all, the Scriptures do not teach baptismal regeneration. The Scriptures do not teach, in other words, that because you are baptized you are saved. Second, the fact that the second birth indicates a birth by God's Spirit explains that the first birth by water, is not of the Spirit, which means it is the natural birth that you and I all know. Let me elaborate upon that for just a moment. I think that Jesus is speaking about a very simple biological truth here. How is the natural man born; What is the first thing that happens when you are born? The placenta ruptures and there is a flow of water and then comes the birth of the natural man. Jesus is trying to drive home to Nicodemus that natural birth comes one way and supernatural birth comes by a different kind of conception. So, He is simply saying to Nicodemus that the natural man is born by water, everybody is born by water. We all have to be born that way. But we must be born again. Verses 7 and 8 are the keys to this passage. Jesus told Nicodemus that the work of the Holy Spirit is like the wind. We can hear it, but we do not know from whence it came or where it is going. All we know is that it has hit us. If God's Spirit is as unpredictable as the wind, then we have to be very careful about not predicting where God is regenerating and where He is not. Never say that there is a man who has listened to the Gospel for ten years and it has not sunk in yet. Do not say that the Spirit cannot be working in him, for God does not run on our timetable. God can be working in a man for twenty years before the Spirit applies the redemption of Christ to that heart and there is supernatural conception.

Flesh produces flesh. Turkeys produce turkeys. Hogs produce hogs. Turtledoves produce turtledovers. You cannot get a camel from a bird. You cannot get a supernatural and spiritual human being from a natural and unbelieving heart. God has to change it. Look at John 16:8-11. "And He, when He comes, (Jesus speaking of the Spirit) will convict the world concerning sin, and righteousness, and judgment; concerning sin, because they do not believe in Me; and concerning righteousness, because I go to the Father, and you no longer

95

behold Me; and concerning judgment, because the ruler of this world has been judged." Three things are listed regarding the Holy Spirit's work: conviction of sin, conviction of righteousness, and conviction of judgment. If you are sure that you have been convicted of those three things, you can be sure that the Spirit that has awakened you is God's Spirit, and not some other spirit. Are you convicted of sin? Do you know you are lost? Are you convicted of righteousness, namely, that God's righteousness in Christ can be imputed to your account by belief? And third, are you convicted that God is a God of judgment and will require from men their deeds, if they are not covered by Christ's blood? Now if you believe those three things, and are confessing Christ as your Savior, you are a joyous person indeed. If you have been born again, you understand these things.

I said at the outset that each member of the Trinity has an integral part in our salvation. What did Got the Father do? What was His major work in your salvation? It was His soveriegn election that you should be one of His children. The second third of your salvation is that Christ came here to die for you specifically. The third part is the Holy Spirit's regenerative work in our hearts awakening us to sin and salvation by application of Christ's blood to our hearts. I wonder if there is a Nicodemus reading this. Are you a teacher of God's people and know not these things? You need to come to Christ. Examine Scripture and see if these things are true for you. If Jesus says, "He who believes in Me shall never perish," believe Him.

THE HOLY CATHOLIC CHURCH
Revelation 5:9

"And they sang a new song, saying, 'Worthy art Thou to take the book, and to break its seals; for Thou wast slain, and didst purchase for God with Thy blood men from every tribe and tongue and people and nation." This verse speaks to the word "catholic". It is a misunderstood phrase because of the existence of the Roman Catholic Church. Looking briefly at the three words, "Holy Catholic Church", we see the following: The word "holy" means separate. The word "catholic" means universal. The word "church", from the Greek "ecclesia", means the called: those who are called to faith in Jesus Christ. So if you have a Holy Catholic Church, you have a Separate Universal Calling. That concept in itself is what the reformers wanted most to make known to the world in their time. I believe it is almost impossible for us to feel what Luther, Calvin, and Beza felt about the dearth of the Roman Catholic Church and its grip upon the world at that time. Calvinism, which is a system of doctrine formulated long after Calvin died, was that which came into conformity with biblical teaching. The Calvinists simply founded their system of doctrine on the Bible. The system of biblical doctrine championed by Calvin's followers became known as Calvinism. The five points of Calvinism, as they are known, are thoroughly biblical. They will

97

help us to fully understand what this separate Universal Calling means. The five points are these: (1) God has chosen for Himself a race of people; (2) Man is totally depraved; (3) Jesus Christ particularly redeemed those whom God had chosen; (4) The way that any of those individuals know that they have been chosen by God is by the Holy Spirit's calling; (5) Once we are saved and in God's hands, there is nothing that we or anybody else can do to change that.

UNCONDITIONAL ELECTION

What this particular point teaches is simply that before God created a thing, there was a book in heaven and its pages were filled with the names of human beings who had not yet been created. Scripture refers to this Book as the "Lamb's Book of Life" and those whose names are in that Book were to be infallibly saved by God throughout the course of world history. I want to make clear at this point, what is commonly misunderstood, that God's election or choice of individuals to be saved has absolutely no bearing upon His foreknowledge of what any individual would do or believe. In other words, God did not look through a crystal ball and say, "In 1975, Bill Jones of the Deerfield Church is going to accept My Son as his Savior; therefore, I will save him." No, the reason that Bill Jones comes to a knowledge of his salvation is the fact that his name is in the Lamb's Book of Life and God is going to bring him to a knowledge of his salvation. Now furthermore, the fact that God chooses anyone unto salvation is what we call grace. But the fact that He chooses particular and certain individuals in what we call sovereign grace. Grace is looser than is sovereign grace. Sovereign grace means that God is not only gracious, but that He is sovereign in that there are particular people who benefit from His saving grace and there are others whom He passes by. Just as much as you would not deny the President the right to invite me to the White House for dinner and not to invite you, neither could any man fault God for saving some and not saving others. God has a right to do this, but someone is going to say, "That's not fair." Let us remember that God's ways are not our ways and we must never subject God's word to our idea of justice. If we were to judge God by what we thought was fair and just, we would rape Scripture beyond any recognition of its being God's Word.

Furthermore, the fact that God is a God of choice, is found all over Scripture. Let me just give you a few illustrations. Israel, the nation, was chosen out of all the other nations. Abraham was chosen to be the head of that race. Jacob and Esau were born from the same womb — one of them was loved, the other one was hated. (Romans 9:6-12) Why was David, the smallest of the sons, the shepherd, chosen to be the king of Israel? What of the disciples? There were plenty of people who lived in Galilee. Why did Jesus Christ pick twelve? God's ways are not our ways. Now let us look quickly at a few verses that will make this clear. If you are a believer, and if you are not, pay particular attention to them as showing that the only way God leads us to a knowledge of His Son is by Scripture. In Ephesians 1:4, Paul says that God has blessed us with every spiritual blessing that we have in Christ. In other words, if you were to draw a list of all the blessings that you have, spiritually speaking, you must trace them back to their source, which is Christ. "Just as He chose us in Him before the foundation of the world, that we should be holy and blameless before Him, in love." God tells us there that "before the foundation of the world" He chose His people and tells us why He did that; that they should be holy (separate), and that they should be blameless. John 15:16 tells us, "You did not choose Me, but I chose you, and appointed you, that you should go and bear fruit, and that your fruit should remain, that whatever you ask of the Father in My name, He may give to you." Then finally in Exodus 33:19, "And He said, 'I Myself will make all My goodness pass before you, and will proclaim the name of the Lord before you; and I will be gracious to whom I will be gracious, and will show compassion on whom I will show compassion.' "

MAN'S TOTAL DEPRAVITY

Now what do we mean when we talk about the total depravity of man? You know what the word "total" means, and "depravity" is that which has so scarred the human race that it cannot do any good to please God. Let us not deduce from this teaching that there is no good in man, because there is good in man. But there is no good in man that will make him acceptable to God. Those are two different things. What did God say to Adam, "In the day you eat of the fruit, you shall surely die."?

When Adam fell, all of Adam fell. He fell from his relationship with God and his body was then put into a position where it could decay. When we speak of total depravity let us not think of the concept that there is no good in anybody, but that man was rendered incapable of pleasing God. All the dimensions of the human race fell. Looking for supportive material in Scripture for the total depravity of man would be no harder than looking for sand at the seashore. Because man fell in sin, he is enslaved to it. We read in Romans 5:12 a verse that can be well illustrated and which, I believe, helps us to understand why we are guilty by inheritance, choice, and enjoyment. We cannot help but sin because we are the seed of Adam. On top of that, we choose to do that which is sin, and to make things worse, we enjoy it! Look at Romans 5:12, "Therefore, just as through one man sin entered into the world, (talking about Adam) and death through sin, so death spread to all men, because all sinned." Adam sinned, Adam died. We all come from Adam, therefore we all sin, therefore we all shall die. It is quite simple.

Let me illustrate that. If I have a beaker of clear water and I have a jar of India ink and I fill an eye dropper with the ink, all I need to do is put one drop of the India ink into the water and it becomes polluted with the ink. There is no way I can take another eye dropper and extract any pure water from the beaker that has now been polluted with the ink. Adam's sin in the human race is analogous to the ink going into the beaker. We are all stained with Adam's sin. Why? Because the Scriptures say so. And the man who does not appreciate Scripture, and does not think God is just, says "That's not fair." But God's ways are not our ways. And if that verse alone sinks into our conscience, our understanding of Scripture will be much easier.

There is another illustration. When the Allied Forces dropped the atomic bombs upon Japan, radioactivity covered the fallen debris and fell upon the people as well. It affected the genetic makeup of the offspring, which means that little children who grew up in Japan and were born after the war closed, in many cases, inherited genetic defects from their parents in a war they had no part in. They did not start the war and yet the effects of it were upon them. It is very much like what happened to us in the fall of Adam. I did not eat from that tree that God forbade Adam to eat, yet I am stained with Adam's sin.

Furthermore, look at Ephesians 2:1-3. If you want a clear-cut and simple verse — indictment of the human race, here you have it. "And you were dead in your trespasses and sins, in which you formerly walked according to the course of this world, according to the prince of the power of the air, of the spirit that is now working in the sons of disobedience. Among them we too all formerly lived in the lusts of our flesh, indulging the desires of the flesh and of the mind, and were by nature children of wrath, even as the rest. As it is written, there is none righteous, not even one. There is none who understands, there is none who seeks for God." (Romans 3:10, 11) "For all have sinned and fall short of the glory of God." (Romans 3:23) "Can the Ethiopian change his skin or the leopard his spots?" (Jeremiah 13:23) What are the answers to those two questions? "No!" We can no more get rid of our sin by ourselves than can a leopard change his spots. That is what God says.

PARTICULAR REDEMPTION

The third point that we are coming to is the most difficult for those who are not thoroughly acquainted with the Scriptures to accept. What does the word "particular" mean? It does not mean "general". Redemption means that God took a step by using His Son, Jesus Christ, to die on a cross to buy back a particular people. This is difficult to understand and therefore we must stay extremely close to Scripture in our understanding of it. Let us just examine two verses, John 3:16 and Romans 3:11. John 3:16 reads: "For God so loved the world, that He gave His only begotten Son, that whoever believes in Him should not perish, but have eternal life." Now granted, that sounds like God has written a blank check. The date, December 25th, is in the upper right corner of the check, it is signed by His own name, but made payable to anyone. That is not what John 3:16 says. Scriptures says that where it says "payable to" all of the names in the Lamb's Book of Life are written on that line. Now how do we know that? How do we know that John 3:16 cannot be a general description of Christ's death? Because of Romans 3:11 which says: "There is none who seeks for God." That means that nobody wants to seek after God; it means nobody can seek after God. That means had you been at the cross of Christ when He died, and the Spirit of God had not been in you to make you aware of what was

101

happening, you would have looked at Him as at any other criminal and you would have walked away and said, "What an awful bloody mess," and it would have had absolutely no impact upon you at all because "No man seeks after God."

Do not tell me, "I sought Christ," because you did not seek Christ. God sought you and by His Spirit drew you to Christ. Let us give God the credit since He is the One who does the seeking. Furthermore, it is easy to understand this a little bit more clearly if we look at it according to Romans 3:11. If you understood John 3:16 as a blank check, that means that Christ would have died for nobody. Why? Well, if no man seeks after God and Christ died for the whole world, that means He would have died for nobody, because nobody would have sought God, nobody could believe in God, so why did Christ die? The design of Christ's death was to redeem, specifically, those whom God had chosen. Scripture shows that this redemption was for many and not all. "For even the Son of Man did not come to be served, but to serve, and to give His life a ransom for many." (Mark 10:45) Not all. How easy it would have been if the Holy Spirit had moved the pen of Mark to have written the word "all" there instead of "many". Jesus, in Matthew 26:28, at the Lord's Supper, speaking to His disciples said, "For this is My blood of the covenant, which is to be shed on behalf of many for forgiveness of sins." Did Jesus Christ goof? Why did He not say "all"? Because that is not what He came to do. He did not come here to die for all men. He came here to die for *His* people. (Matthew 1:21) "And they shall call His Name Immanuel, and He shall save His people from their sins." It is a *particular* group which makes the doctrine of the cross all that more precious to us who believe. He is *our* Christ.

We have seen that God has chosen a people. We have seen that those He has chosen along with the rest of the human race have been completely depraved. We have seen that Christ came to die specifically for God's people. Now so far, that means nothing as far as our belief is concerned. We must be effectually called.

EFFECTUAL CALLING

What does the word "effectual" mean? You know that the word "ineffectual" means something that does not work. Effectual calling is the teaching that God's Holy Spirit infallibly makes every single person for whom Christ died aware of it. The only reason you are aware of the fact that you are a Christian is because God's Spirit has come into your heart and has cried, "Abba, Father" and has led you to the truth of Christ. Otherwise, you would not know Him. Why? Because Romans 3:11 says, "No man seeks after God." God's election of us, and Christ's redemption for us, still would not make us seek after God. It takes the Holy Spirit to cause us to see Christ. "For all who are being led by the Spirit of God, these are sons of God." (Romans 8:14) In other words, you cannot be a son of God unless the Holy Spirit has led you to that position. Before we leave this point, let us turn to the most conclusive set of verses. John 6 really makes it clear. It makes it so clear that those who are still struggling with these verses will not like them. I can remember when I did not like these verses. I love them now. John 6:37 reads, "All that the Father gives Me shall come to Me; and the one who comes to Me I will certainly not cast out." What does the first part of the verse say? It says that the Father has a group of people that He has given to Christ. Are they not God's chosen? Yes. And did not Christ die for them? Now go down the page to verse 44: "No one can come to Me, unless the Father who sent Me draws him; and I will raise him up on the last day." Verse 45 reads: "It is written in the prophets, 'And they shall all be taught of God.' Every one who has heard and learned from the Father, comes to Me." Then verses 64 and 65: " 'But there are some of you who do not believe.' For Jesus knew from the beginning who they were who did not believe, and who it was that would betray Him. And He was saying, 'For this reason I have said to you, that no one can come to Me, unless it has been granted him from the Father.' " Now how clear can God make it that no man can come to Christ unless the Spirit draws him? We cannot come on our own and all of those who do come to Christ come to Him because the Father has led them to Christ. And when they get to Christ, what does Christ say? "I will in no wise cast them out." Why will Christ in no wise cast you out if you come to Him? Because the Father has given you to the Son! Can the Son be disobedient to the Father and cast you out? Hardly!

ETERNAL SECURITY

The fifth point is the most securing. It is the doctrine of

eternal security. It is also known as the doctrine of the "perseverance of the saints." In short: once saved, always saved. The Holy Spirit prods us to obey God; He does not permit us to fall from God. "For I am confident of this very thing, that He who began a good work in you will perfect it until the day of Christ Jesus." (Philippians 1:6) That means when God plows a field, He intends to plant seeds in it, and when God plants a seed it will grow. And when God comes into your life and makes you aware of your salvation, it means that you are in His hands forever. That is what Jesus means when He says, "No man can pluck them out of My hand." How can you possibly wriggle your way out of God's hand when He says, "You are Mine"? He will not let go. If Christ's blood was shed for you, how can He let you go? Can we unchoose ourselves? Of course not. Can we ask Christ to die again, not just for us, but for the whole world? No. God has said that Christ came here for His people; we cannot undo that. How are we going to uncall ourselves? The Holy Spirit has effectually called us to faith. If *God* has saved us, how could we unsave ourselves? If God is Almighty and is powerful and saved us, how can we, who are weak, possibly undo what God has done?

This is the holy catholic church. This is the separate, universal calling of God. Separate because God has made us separate by His sovereign grace. Universal, not because all men are saved, but universal because God saves some Japanese, God saves some Germans, God saves some Samoans, God saves some Russians, God saves some Chinese, etc. Not one tribe, tongue or nation shall be unrepresented in heaven because God said so in Revelation 5:9. When we say the Apostles' Creed, that is what we say we believe. "I believe in the holy catholic church." I believe that is the way we are saved because the Bible says it. Are you a believer? Has the Holy Spirit called you to faith? God says, "If you hear My voice, obey," and God says that if you come to Him, Christ will in no wise cast you out. Is the Holy Spirit effectually calling you? Has He plowed a number of furrows in your life recently? Has He planted some seeds there? Do you feel the wind of the Spirit coming and going? Believe on the Lord Jesus Christ and you shall be saved! And when you are saved, you shall give God the glory, you will not say to yourself, "I saved myself, what a lucky man am I that I chose Christ." You will know from God's Word that you never sought Christ. You would have killed Him if you could. Will you come?

"THE COMMUNION OF SAINTS"
Romans 1:8, 9

The Church at Rome developed in a way which is not anywhere recorded in Scripture. We know that Rome was the capitol of the ancient world and we know that Paul wrote the Epistle to the Romans because he was shortly expecting to visit the Church there. If we look at verses 8 and 9 of the first chapter of Romans we read: "First, I thank my God through Jesus Christ for you all, because your faith is being proclaimed throughout the whole world. For God, whom I serve in my spirit in the preaching of the gospel of His Son, is my witness as to how unceasingly I make mention of you." Not only had Paul not been to Rome, but reports had come back to him from this church that the Church in Rome was alive and well.

Not all men can say what Paul says here in verse 8. "First, I thank my God." The fact that the personal pronoun "my" is there is indicative of the fact that there is a personal relationship not only between him and God, but between him and those to whom he is writing who also profess the Lord Jesus Christ as their God. The "you all" is indicative of that as well. Paul is thanking God here at the outset for spiritual growth in a Church he has not seen. Are we not thankful for letters that we receive from our missionaries in the field about the progress that is being made in individuals who are being led to the Lord, even though we have not seen these people?

The first cohesive element of the communion of the saints which I believe that we can glean from these two verses is prayer. Prayer is a very important cohesive element to the communion of the saints. We are commanded to pray for one another. We are commanded to pray for all men, and yet much of our prayers are dumb because prayers go up to the throne of grace either for the wrong motive or they are prayed without the intercession of Jesus Christ or we pray for things which God has strictly forbidden. So a prayer from the non-believer is ineffective. There is a story of a chapel in a little Belgium town during World War II named Ostende which prostitutes frequented to ask God for good health. Those are the kinds of prayers which bounce off walls and ceilings. You cannot expect God to answer your prayer if it is asked for a wrong motive or if it is asked unscripturally or if it is certainly asking for something that God has forbidden. If you see division in a certain church or in a certain family, you can be sure that there is a lack of cohesive effective prayer in that particular group. God listens to effective prayer. James tells us that "the fervent prayer of a righteous man does much," and where we see very little done, we can know that effective prayer is missing. It is an indispensable element of the communion of the saints.

The second element which we glean from this passage is faith. What does Paul say in verse 8? "I thank God," for what? "For you all, because your faith is being proclaimed throughout the whole world." Now this is the same kind of understanding that Paul uses later on in the first chapter, down in verses 16, 17 and 18, where the righteousness of God is revealed by faith to faith, witness to witness, mouth to mouth. That is the second thing that cannot be lost. Can we say that of our own congregation? Can we say that we have a voice proclaiming Christ to all nations? If we are going to be a congregation which demonstrates the community of the saints, then we have to be prayerfully effective, and we have to know that our faith is known not just within the bounds of these four walls, but within the bounds of New Jersey, the east coast of the United States, Mexico, Nepal and other places.

Love is the third element. The kind of love Paul is talking about here is impersonal but genuine. You will notice in verse 9, "For God, whom I serve in my spirit in the preaching of the gospel of His Son, is my witness as to how unceasingly I make mention of you." Paul loved the Church of Rome. He had never met them, yet he loved them. It is interesting to me that we are able to love Christians even though we do not know them. No Christian has the same character makeup; yet, in Christ we are one. We see from Peter's writings later on in the Epistles that he was a man of faith and love.

Now someone is going to ask, "What in capsule form is the meaning of the phrase 'the communion of saints'?" It is the Unity of the believers. We are chosen by God the Father, redeemed by Christ, and regenerated spiritually by the Holy Spirit. That means that we have one God, one faith and one Gospel to preach. When we break out of the bounds of those things, we find we become quickly disunified. The section of the Apostles' Creed that we are in now gives us a very sure knowledge of our salvation. I would like you to turn to two verses which are very important to our understanding of the communion of the saints. I John 3:14 is the first one, and I close with the element of love here by this particular verse. "We know that we have passed out of death into life, because we love the brethren. He who does not love abides in death." Now you see there are very few Scriptures in the Bible, very few verses in the Bible, where you really can test your spiritual life. If you go into a hardware store and buy a battery, they have a tester there by which you can determine if you are buying a good battery. If you want to check out your spiritual status before God there are some verses in the Bible which will help, and here is one of them. If you really have no love for the brethren, you ought to question whether or not you are really born again. I am not talking along denominational lines. I mean anyone who confesses the Lord Jesus Christ and believes in his heart that God raised Christ from the dead. I have shaken hands with a man who was the leader of a gang in New York City and is now a renowned black evangelist. I have also shaken hands with a little man by the name of Manuel, down in the Tarascan Indians in Mexico who has no idea what New York City is all about, who if he were to see an electric pencil sharpener or an electric can opener would be ecstatic with amazement. Here are two men on opposite sides of the globe, who are in two different cultures, two different backgrounds, and yet there is an affinity there that no man can destroy. They both know Christ as their Savior, they both know they must obey Him, they both know they must love the brethren. How is that possible? Where can they get that kind of information? How can Manuel, an illiterate Tarascan Indian and a fellow like Tom Skinner arrive at the same conclusions about what it means to be in communion with the saints? It is done by the Spirit's work in their lives and done in conjunction with the study of the Scriptures.

Now the question always arises, "What about those who seem to be one of us, but then defect or leave the fold?" What about those we talk about when we say, "We thought they were Christians, they confessed Christ, and now they have gone out"? There is a very interesting verse in Scripture which may answer that question for us. It is I John 2:19. It reads: "They went out from us, but they were not really of us; for if they had been of us, they would have remained with us; but they went out, in order that it might be shown that they all are not of us." You have to be very careful when you read a verse like this. It does not mean that because someone has become inactive in your church he is not a Christian or has rejected Christ or the Gospel. But it does mean that in some instances, where those who said they were one of our number and then rejected our number, even rejected Christ Himself and the Gospel, the reason is that they were never Christ's in the first place. Any man or woman who has a thorough knowledge of Scripture knows that you cannot be born again one day and lost again another. If you are born again, you will love the brethren. If you are born again, you will recognize the communion of the saints. But if you are not born again these things do not mean anything to you at all and never did. The day comes when you suddenly realize you are kidding yourself and off you go. Now that covers the first part of the discussion by definition of the communion of the saints. Three cohesive elements must be there: love, faith and discipline, as well as a recognition of the fact that God is able to work on others the same miracle which He has worked in your life and that He has worked in others.

If you will turn to a second passage in the book of Romans, we will turn the coin of this particular phrase of the Apostles' Creed. Look at the last chapter of Romans, chapter 16, verses 17 and 18. "Now I urge you, brethren, keep your eye on those who cause dissensions and hindrances contrary to the teaching which you learned, and turn away from them. For such men are slaves not of our Lord Christ but of their own appetites; and by their smooth and flattering speech they deceive the hearts of the unsuspecting." I do not believe you can effectively study this doctrine without looking at what it means to look at those who are divisive in the Church of Christ. In the Greek this expression, "keep your own eye", is the Greek verb "scopane" from which we get our English derivative of microscope and telescope. Obviously, any denial of the person of Christ or of His work is heresy. If a man or a woman denies that Jesus Christ is the Incarnate Son of God raised from the dead, or denies that His central work was to die for the sins of His people, such a person is not a believer. Jesus Christ died as a payment for our sins. He did not die to set any example for us. He lived to teach, but He did not die to set an example. Dissensions in the Church are very hard to detect, and the reason they are hard to detect is because they lie right alongside the truth. They look just like the truth. They have the same color, they have the same feeling, and you can get ministers of the Gospel of Christ who can preach heresy as effectively as ministers can preach truth.

The first kind of dissension that we have discussed is that about heresy. It is hard to detect, but it is rare also. The other kind that is much more prevalent is that of legalistic ignorance. For instance, you cannot find a verse in Scripture anywhere which says to take a drink is a sin. You cannot find a verse in Scripture anywhere which says to be a member of the United Presbyterian Church is a sin, and yet I have been called a sinner on that account.

Last summer, when I was on my vacation, I was asked to speak in the pulpit of an independent Bible Baptist Church. I preached a few sermons there while the minister was away. When he returned he invited me over to his house for some ice cream and a chat by the fireside. The first thing he said to me was, "Do you realize the trouble you've caused by preaching here?" And I said, "No, what happened?" He said, "Well, a family left our Church because you came here and preached." I asked, "Is that good or bad?" And he replied, "I think it's good." The reason that the family left was because a man was occupying their pulpit who did not believe in immersion. I was not even heard. Someone left that Church because a heretic was coming to preach who did not cross his t's and dot his i's just the way that one Christian family did. That is a classical example of the kind of thing that causes dissension in the Church of Jesus Christ. You know, if you have ever had any opportunity to oversee a group of people doing a specific job, how bickering between the individuals who are trying to get the job done is a constant pain in the neck to the individual whose job it is to see that the job gets done. I have mental visions of God in heaven looking down upon His Church and seeing that 99% of the time they are needling each other about whether or not they cross their t's and dot their i's the way others do. That is the reason why the man on the street is not impressed with most evangelists. Everywhere they look they see a Baptist calling a Presbyterian a heretic; they see a Presbyterian calling a Baptist a heretic because he immerses instead of sprinkling, and back and forth it goes. That kind of business has no place in the Church of Jesus Christ. We are commanded to study Scripture and if it is Scriptural, it is right.

You also get people in the Church who say of the minister, "Oh, he is a faithful man, but I don't know where he is going, so I will stand off and watch." Then you get a dissension by default because you get individuals who will not commune with each other and move in the same direction for Christ's sake, but you have one standing on the sidelines who says, "Well, I don't want to affiliate with them too closely; after all, I don't think they are right on this issue." So the troops become divided and the battle does not get won. Do you know what God says about these people? He says, "Keep an eye on them, watch them." We must do that. These are those people who serve their own appetites, as Paul says here, they do not serve Christ. They are more interested in your mode of baptism and your view of escatology then they are with Christ. They are dangerous people; keep your eye on them!

Now note what the Scripture says about how to handle

these people. I am constantly amazed, as I study the Scripture, what God's answer is for dissension in the Church. God's answer is to *avoid* them. God does not want His children flirting with those who are more interested in dissension then with the unity of the believers. Now I think there is a caution here also. Turn to II Thessalonians 3:13-15. "But as for you, brethren, do not grow weary of doing good. And if anyone does not obey our instruction in this letter, take special note of that man and do not associate with him, so that he may be put to shame. And yet do not regard him as an enemy, but admonish him as a brother.' " So what do you do with individuals in your Church who say you are not crossing your t's and dotting your i's according to their standards? You rebuke them in love, if they are scripturally wrong. You pray for them. Then here is the very important principle which I want all of us to know: *take issue with the problem, not the person!* I talk to legalists all the time. They drive me crazy. But the way you deal with them is to deal with the issue, not with the person. Just keep passing the person by and deal with the issue. "Show me Scripture." I say. "Show me Scripture, show me Scripture." Do not call them eggheads or fatheads and walk away from them. That never accomplishes anything. Just tell them to show you Scripture, and if they can do that you are wrong, admit it.

In conclusion, let me say that the communion of the saints depends upon sound doctrine. The division of the saints comes from unsound doctrine. The communion of the saints happens when our appetite is for Christ, not for ourselves. Division in the Church comes very quickly when our appetites become our own standard of what is right or wrong. Are we praying for those things that are unifying in the Church of Jesus Christ? Are we really? Look around you. Think of the people that you know in our Church. Do they see everything the way you do? Of course they don't. So what do you do when they do not see things your way? Scoff at them? Walk away from them? Call them names? That is not the remedy. If they are wrong according to Scripture, rebuke them in love and pray for them. But if they are not wrong, and if you cannot show them Scripture to show them they are wrong, forget it. You have a Gospel to preach, you have souls to bring to Christ. We are not going to do that by taking each other's glasses off and seeing if they are clean enough for us.

But if you are a non-believer, you do not have any communion at all, do you? You do not even know what it means to be a brother or a sister in Christ. You do not have a family. So I invite you to search Scripture on that account and see if the Lord Jesus Christ is the Son of God. Is He the One that has been promised to come and redeem you from your sins? Is He capable of changing your life? So to the believer, let us search Scripture to see if we are right before we speak. For non-believers, let them search the Scriptures to see if Christ is to be their Lord.

"THE FORGIVENESS OF SINS"
I John 1:9

In I John 1:6-10 we read, "If we say that we have fellowship with Him and yet walk in the darkness, we lie and do not practice the truth; but if we walk in the light as He Himself is in the light, we have fellowship with one another, and the blood of Jesus His Son cleanses us from all sin. If we say we have no sin, we are deceiving ourselves, and the truth is not in us." Jesus Christ is not in your life if you believe that you do not sin. "If we confess our sin, He is faithful and righteous to forgive us our sins and to cleanse us from all unrighteousness. If we say that we have not sinned, we make Him a liar, and His word is not in us."

The portion of the Apostles' Creed that we are studying here is that we believe in the forgiveness of sins. Verse 8 tells us that the denial that sin exists in our nature can only come from a non-believer's heart. Verse 10 shows that any denial that sin manifests itself in our nature anywhere is also a denial of the fact that Christ can be in you. But verse 9 is the antidote for the emergence of sin in our lives. It is confession. Here is what your attitude about sin is to be. Admit that you have it in you, and admit that you do it. That is the first step from darkness into light. As soon as you realize that you are a sinner and that it

113

condemns you and that you need Christ to be delivered from it, you are taking the first steps by the prompting of the Holy Spirit to move in the direction of what is called the new birth.

God does two things if we confess our sins. He removes the guilt and He reinstates us to fellowship with Him. The guilt is cleared because of the blood of Christ that has been shed, but also the vestiges of disfellowship are washed away. Furthermore, we know that He is faithful to do it. You see, there are no clauses that we find in these verses which show that God would be an unwilling or unjust forgiver. Let us turn to an Old Testament verse which makes it quite clear of the promise that God made through Jeremiah. Look at Jeremiah 31:34. "And they shall not teach again, each man his neighbor and each man his brother, saying, "Know the Lord," for they shall all know Me, from the least of them to the greatest of them,' declares the Lord, 'for I will forgive their iniquity, and their sin I will remember no more.' " That is the glorious part of the forgiveness of sins. God does not remember, on confession, the sin that you have just committed. He does not store it away to bring it back and bother you with it years later when you are getting out of line. It is gone, forgiven, forgotten, forever!

Now let us look at the two major subdivisions of this context. The first is that there is a divine dilemma here. How can a just God, who is holy and demands holy activity upon our part justify or clear the sinner? If God is just and cannot come into contact with sinners, let alone invite them into His heaven, what is it that must take place so that God can have fellowship with an unrighteous sinner like myself and like you? The second division is to see the marvel of His faithfulness. Let us look first at the divine dilemma.

Whether you know it or not, your soul fears God when you sin. The Christian who sins fears God, not in the sense that he will be judged, but in the sense that he has grieved the Christ who has died for him. When the non-Christian sins, he feels the guilt that the man felt that Paul is talking about in Romans 1:18-25. All men know there is a God. Show me a man who says he is an agnostic and I will show you a man who is a liar. Yet there are millions of people who say, "I know there is a God, but I refuse to honor Him as God," and they turn away from Him, serving their own lusts and other gods. It is that particular individual who falls under the category of the individual who knows he is guilty when he sins. Adam and Eve's first reaction following their sin was to run from God and hide some place where no one would see them. There are cities and nations and even people of history who have borne this particular truth out. Sodom, Ninevah, Tyre, Babylon, and Sidon all felt the heavy dark cloud of God's judgment hanging over them. Nineveh repented and Babylon did in a sense, but then of course fell away. Nebuchadnezzar, from what we can tell in the book of Daniel, was somehow put into a right relationship with God, although I do not fully understand what the Scripture says there about him. Sodom certainly did not repent. Tyre and Sidon, which were at one time the two greatest seaports in the Mediterranean Sea, are today little broken-down Arab towns. All of them historically have fallen under God's judgment. Every transgression that a man makes against God's Law produces guilt. And what he does with that guilt is what the natural man does, according to Romans 1. He sins against a holy God, even though he knows God. Because he is not honoring God as the Creator, he can only do one thing with his guilt. Instead of laying it at the feet of the Savior and asking Him for forgiveness, the only other thing he can do with it is to tuck it under his arm like a football carrier would do with a football and run from God as fast as he can, hoping that the judgment will not fall upon him and hoping that God will not find the sin. But the guilt that is there and the tendency to run from the Holy God is in every man.

For the believer particularly, justice is no longer our enemy. Yet, justice is the enemy of many. If a man says, "I'll take my chances with God; if He'll be just with me, I'll be satisfied." But you would not be satisfied; because if God is just with you, He will send you to hell, because that is His only alternative. How can a Holy God let you into His heaven? His holy justice is assuaged by His putting a substitute in your place. So that instead of your having to die for your sins and being condemned for them, God's own Son stepped into that place for you. By faith in Him you go free. But the man who insists on taking his chances before the judgment seat of God and will not let Christ be his substitute receives his just deserts.

Now, if you love sin, if you really love it and serve it, there is no hope for you to be pardoned as long as you are in that attitude. Christians sin, but no Christian loves sin. The Scriptures teach us that when the Spirit of Christ is in us, He cries "Abba, Father", and we are led to repentance. We may sin and we may become hardened of heart at times, but as children of God we do not serve sin. The non-Christian not only serves sin, but he enjoys it.

Now, justice has been satisfied by substitution. The Old Testament prepared us for understanding that Jesus was to be a vicarious sacrifice. By vicarious I mean substitutionary. That is what the word means. In the Old Testament, if Mr. Smith killed a man, he had to die for that sin. Nobody else could take his place. It is quite clear in the ordinances and ceremonial law of the Old Testament that whoever the particular person was who had committed the sin, he personally, had to pay for it. If two men strive with one another and a woman who is pregnant happens to get bumped in the course of the fight and she has a miscarriage, the man who started the fight must pay the husband of the woman a certain amount of money for damage. He had to do it *personally*. Harry Jones who lives next door cannot step in and say, "I will pay the debt." The man who did it had to pay the debt. The Old Testament prepared us very well for this. So, that that means, according to New Testament theology, that as a sinner, which you are, you must stand before God personally and face Him. Nobody else can take your place, humanly speaking. And because you cannot find anyone else to take your place, and because you cannot face God and justify yourself, the choice is to either be condemned, or trust in the substitute God has provided. Jesus Christ stood in your place and died for you. Now, the Scriptures teach us that He died. The just died for the unjust in order that He might bring us to God. This word "just" is an important word. In the Greek it is "dikaios" which is also the same Greek word for "righteous". So when God says you must be righteous, He is saying you must be just. "And when I justify you," says God, "I make you as righteous."

What happens when Jesus Christ, the substitute, dies for us, the sinner? His righteousness becomes our righteousness. It is important to note the relationship of Jesus Christ to the Father concerning all of this. It was Jesus Christ who was

116

judged guilty. If you turn to the Old Testament you will see a passage in Isaiah 53 which makes it clear that God the Father Almighty was happy about the fact that Jesus Christ was killed for you and me. Do not let anyone ever tell you that Jesus Christ went to the cross begrudgingly, or went to the cross in a different attitude than the Father had in store for Him. "This Man, delivered up by the predetermined plan and foreknowledge of God, you nailed to the cross by the hands of godless men and put Him to death." (Acts 2:23) Isaiah 53:10 says, "But the Lord was pleased to crush Him, putting Him to grief; if He would render Himself as a guilt offering, He will see His offspring, He will prolong His days, and the good pleasure of the Lord will prosper in His hand." That simply means this: That after He had been falsely accused by the Jewish hierarchy, after Herod had falsely accused Him, after Pilate had judged Him, God was still unsatisfied. God was only satisfied when He killed His own Son for you and me. It is important to realize that the suffering of Christ in our place did not precede the 'cross. Christ's life, the ignominious way of His life, His abuse by people, is not what liberates us from our sin. It was His death that paid the penalty. The fact that Jesus Christ had a sinless life is what made Him eligible to go to the cross. But what actually removes our guilt was His death. Christ's life on this earth prior to the cross has nothing to do with saving you by removing your guilt. It simply made Him eligible to die as a sinless being.

Let us look at the second major division here. The first was that God has provided a way for us to become cleared of our guilt by having a substitute die for us. The second part of the verse is comforting. We are here taught that every time a redeemed sinner confesses his sin, it will be forgiven. It never fails. Why? Because God has given His Word that it will always be that way. I do not care what you have done. If you confess your sins, Christ will forgive them. You say, "I've blasphemed. God will not forgive me." Yes, he will. You say, "I've committed adultery, God will not forgive that sin." Yes, He will. Romans 8:26 also bears on this subject. The question is asked, "If I confess my sin, God is faithful and just to forgive me; but what if I should commit a terrible sin and end up like Karen Quinlin and go into a coma and die before I can confess my sin?" There is an answer for that in Scripture. Look at Romans 8:26. "And in the same way the Spirit also helps our weakness; for we do not know how to pray as we should, but the Spirit Himself intercedes for us with groanings too deep for words." That does not mean we are to stop confessing sin and that the Spirit in us somehow automatically intercedes for us, but it means that the Holy Spirit will do what we cannot do. God knows us, He has made us, He remembers that we are dust, He knows that we are frail. We are to confess our sins and we are to be diligent in it; but how marvelous it is to know that the Spirit who is in us intercedes for us with words we do not and cannot utter. That is a marvelous comfort to me. There is a story about Charles Wesley, when he was in this country many, many years ago preaching. He had a close friend by the name of Joseph, who was a carrier for him, and Wesley always asked him to mail letters. Wesley at that time was courting a lady in England who at first did not want to come to Georgia, but did come later for one trip. Just before one of his evening services, Wesley said to Joseph. "Joseph, I want you to take these letters down to the post and have them mailed." And Joseph said, "No sir, I'll go after you preach." And Wesley said, "You'll go now," but Joseph said, "I will not." Wesley said. "You realize this means there must be a parting of our company." Joseph said, "If that is what it must be, then that is what it must be." So both of them slept on it and both of them got up at four o'clock in the morning to continue the conversation. Wesley said to Joseph, "Are you ready to ask forgiveness?" And Joseph replied, "No, I'm not." Wesley said, "Well, I hope you are ready to forgive me." The relationship was reinstated immediately. Wesley knew the Scriptures well enough to know that pride is the biggest barrier to asking forgiveness. Wesley loved this individual so much that he would do anything to keep him in his company. God loves you so much that He has provided a way for you to come to Him any time you sin. He wants you to do it and He says that when you do He will always be faithful to forgive you.

If you are a believer in the Lord Jesus Christ, do you know what you need to do? You need first to realize you are a sinner who is deserving of damnation. Second, you need to realize is that God has provided a substitute for you and that you need not face Him as a judge. Then you need to fully believe that the blood of the Lord Jesus Christ shed upon the cross covers all your sin. Then you need to say, "Lord Jesus, You save me, because I cannot save myself." Sin is anything that falls short of God's standards.

Tell me, have you really lived today perfectly? Has God been delighted with everything you have done and everything you have said? Stop trying to get to God through some other means than Christ, because He will not let you in.

"THE RESURRECTION OF THE BODY"
Philippians 3:21

The reason that it is important to believe in the resurrection of the body is simply that if we deny the resurrection of our own bodies, we must also deny the resurrection of Christ. Had He not been raised from the dead, He would not be at the right hand of the Father now, so we would not only not have a risen Savior, but we would not have a High Priest either. Our salvation will not be complete until we receive our new bodies. "For our citizenship is in heaven, from which also we eagerly wait for a Savior, the Lord Jesus Christ; who will transform the body of our humble state into conformity with the body of His glory, by the exertion of the power that He has even to subject all things to Himself." (Philippians 3:20) The verse teaches us four things: (1) Our citizenship is in heaven; (2) God will raise the bodies of His own children; (3) they will be like Christ's risen body; (4) He is able to do that by the power of His own resurrection.

Now the Scriptures teach a literal resurrection. It teaches us that if we are the heirs of Christ, we are to be raised with a body like His. That means that the body that Christ had when He was raised from the dead is very similar to that which you and I and any other believer will have. It is interesting when you turn to the Gospel of John and are reading the narrative there about Jesus' conversation with Mary and Martha about the death of their brother Lazarus. "Martha said to Him, 'I know that he will rise again in the resurrection on the last day.'" (John 11:24) There is proof from Scripture that a pre-New Testament Jew believed in the resurrection of the dead. It is taught in the Old Testament in various portions of Scripture. It was common belief, not only among Jews, but among pagans.

We know from Scripture that only the body knows the grave. There is no such thing as "soul sleep". I have said that our bodies will be like the post-resurrection body of Jesus Christ. Let us not spend a lot of time in foolish speculation about what we are going to look like. It is wonderful enough to know that we are going to have our bodies raised, but more importantly, that they will be like Christ's. It is also important to see that the semblance of our new body will have to be something like our present bodies because otherwise it would not be called a resurrection, it would be called a recreation. Let us look at the miracle that the Lord is going to perform. The text here in Philippians 3:21 says that we have a body of a humble estate. What does that mean? The Greek word here means that we have a body now which is incapable of inheriting glory. We have a body now which is incapable of inheriting heaven.

God is going to give us a new body for two reasons. The first is that the vestiges of this body which is used to sinning and which is stained with the sin of a fallen race must be done away with. That is why our bodies must undergo corruption. (The Spirit does not go through corruption if one is in Christ.) Now the Lord also had a humiliated body. It perspired, it bled and it suffered pain, sorrow, and emotional turmoil like you and I do. That body was transformed into a different kind and yet the disciples recognized Christ after He revealed Himself to them. Anything that your body now suffers, or anything that your body now has which causes discomfort is just not going to be there in the resurrected body, because the Scriptures teach us that there will be no pain and every tear shall be wiped from our eyes. If you look at I John 3:2, you have the clearest statement in Scripture, which teaches that our body will be like

Christ's. I John 3:2 reads: "Beloved, now we are children of God, and it has not appeared as yet what we shall be. We know that, when He appears, we shall be like Him, because we shall see Him just as He is." That teaches us that Christ will be seen as He is and that our body will be very much like His. Look also at I Corinthians 15:51. "Behold, I tell you a mystery; we shall not all sleep, but we shall all be changed." That simply means that when the Lord Jesus Christ returns to take His Church home, there is going to be a lot of people on this earth who are His believers who are alive. Their bodies will go through an instantaneous corruption and also an instantaneous transformation. So whether we are talking about the body of an individual which is lying in a cemetery or whether we are talking about your body tonight if Christ should return, your body, as have the ones in a cemetery, must suffer corruption, as your body in its present state cannot enter into God's holy heaven.

Furthermore, our present bodies hinder us from proper worship. We have aches, we have pains, we have joy, we have sorrow. We have all kinds of things which distract us from God and worship. Those things hinder our fellowship with other Christians and hinder our fellowship in corporate worship. The miracle of the new body is amazing enough, but it is not more amazing than the spiritual resurrection that I talked about earlier. Think about it. Is it any more a miracle for God to raise up a body than to regenerate a soul? The fact that man, who hates God and does not know God, is brought to a knowledge of God is a miracle. I just want to make it clear to you that when we talk about the resurrection of the body, we are not talking about anything more stupendous than when we say an individual is become born again or brought to a knowledge of his salvation.

There are some who are worried about the condition of the body in regard to how it is disposed after death. What about those who have cremated? Their bodies have gone up in ashes and floated off into the air. How is God going to raise a new body from that? What about bones that have disintegrated in the earth? What about Christians who were torn to pieces by beasts in Roman arenas? How can God raise a body from something like that? That is no problem for God. There is an interesting verse in Scripture which teaches us that it is no problem for God. First of all, God made man from dust. To dust our bodies return. Yet that does not cancel the power of God. "And He is before all things, and in Him all things hold together." (Colossians 1:17) That means that molecular and atomic structures are under Christ's control. They are commanded into existence and are maintained by His Word. He is the key to the universe physically as well as spiritually. For God to call back the atoms and the molecules of a body that was cremated or eaten or crushed or dismembered is no more difficult for God than to take dust and make a body out of that.

Finally, let us see the power which will do this. What does Philippians 3:21 say? It tells us there will be a resurrection of the body and it tells us that our bodies will be like the body of His glory. But how is it going to happen? By the exertion of the power that He has, even to subject all things unto Himself. 'Well," you say, "How is it going to happen?" First of all, when Jesus Christ raises the dead it will be as a risen Savior come with power. We read in Romans 8:28-30, "Those whom He predestined and foreknew, He also called and when He called He justified; those whom He justified He sanctified and those whom He sanctified He glorified." Glorification, reception of the new and glorified body is the last step. Those of us who are believers have been called, chosen, and justified. We are being sanctified but we have not yet been glorified. That does not happen until we lose this body and gain the new one, which Philippians 3:21 said, is like the body of His glory. Now that is the marvelous truth of the last step of the salvation which is ours. Were we not to have a new body, our salvation would just simply be incomplete. Adam lost more than you might think in the "fall". What happened when he sinned? He lost his spiritual relationship with God. He lost his intellect, and his body died. But when we are regenerated, our spirits are put back into right relationship with God. Our intellect is restored in that we have the mind of Christ. Then our bodies have to be saved also. They were all lost, but God will save them all for His own children and without it our salvation is not complete.

It is true also that if no man can resist the physical resurrection of the body, then no man can resist the spiritual resurrection either. That means if you are not a believer in Christ, you have no more ability to resist His call to you than does the believer have the ability to resist having a new body. I think that is important for us to know, because God will use all means to bring His elect to a knowledge of Himself. He may use war, He may use famine, He may cause you to lose your job, He may cause you to lose your wife or your children. God will do anything to bring you to a knowledge of the Savior, Jesus Christ, if you are His child. That is a marvelous truth, because the burden of saving yourself is removed from you, as you cannot do it. Do you feel the Spirit of Christ in you, prodding you to examine these truths? Look at the kinds of people in Scripture that Jesus subdued. There was Zaccheus. Jesus subdued him. He said, "Zaccheus, come down." That was it! Zaccheus came down and was conquered. Nicodemus had questions for Jesus which probably none of the other Pharisees that he talked to were able to answer. Jesus answered the question and subdued Nicodemus. The woman of Samaria was subdued, and He can subdue you. He will subdue you if you are His.

Now if the point of this text is that God will change a vile body into a glorious one, He can also change a vile spirit into one that is acceptable to Him.

Before we close, look at Job 19:26. "Even after my skin is flayed, (or rotten) yet in my flesh I shall see God." And if you have written, in your translation, "without flesh I shall see God," that refers to "without this" flesh. When the Scriptures say that in my flesh I shall see God, that obviously means you are going to have a new body. That is the whole point of that verse. "I know that my redeemer liveth and I shall see Him standing in the latter day and I shall see Him in my flesh." We must believe in the resurrection of the body because Scripture teaches it. If we do not believe in that, we are not going to believe in the resurrection of our own Lord, and without that we are lost. If He is dead, then so is God's provision for our salvation dead. As Paul says, "We are of all men most to be pitied. But now Christ has been raised from the dead, the first fruits of those who are asleep." (I Corinthians 15:19b, 20)

"AND THE LIFE EVERLASTING. AMEN."
John 10:27-29

In my closing year of student assistantship to Dr. James M. Boice at the Tenth Presbyterian Church in Philadelphia, Pennsylvania, before the Lord called me to Deerfield Street, a very interesting thing happened. Dr. Boice was preaching from the Gospel of John in a lengthy series. When preaching through chapters 6-10, a few listeners who still clung to the flesh's worth in salvation made it known that they had had enough of Calvinism. On one of the pews after one of these particular services somebody had scribbled in bold print on the bulletin, "I am sick of Calvinism." His response in succeeding weeks was to press the Doctrine of Calvin all the harder. Calvinism is that system of doctrine which embraces biblical theology. Calvin would say that he was an Augustinian. Augustine would say he was Pauline. Paul would have certainly said he was Christian. If you are a Calvinist, you believe Scripture to be the Word of God. If you believe in the doctrines that the Scriptures teach and that God is a sovereign God and is in complete control of this world and the salvation of His people, you are a Calvinist whether you know it or not.

We are presently in John, chapter 10. No matter how many denominations there are, God has divided the world into two groups: sheep and goats. If you are a Christian, you are a sheep. You are one of God's children. Let us see that in these verses Jesus is contrasting the state of the elect versus the state of the non-elect, and that the elect of God hear His voice and that the call to them by the Spirit is as irresistible as was Christ's call to Lazarus. Our outline has three headings: (1) The relationship of CHrist to the sheep; (2) The lost condition of the non-elect; (3) The relationship of grace to everlasting life; (4) How the sheep hear; (5) Eternal life is a gift of God.

Our text reads, "My sheep hear My voice, and I know them, and they follow Me; and I give eternal life to them, and they shall never perish; and no one shall snatch them out of My hand. My Father, who has given them to Me, is greater than all; and no one is able to snatch them out of the Father's hand." What is the relationship between Christ and the sheep? The sheep were given to Christ by the Father. We are told that in John 6:37. Christ died for the sheep, therefore they belong to Him. (10:15) The way that the sheep come to the knowledge of the fact that they are in the fold and that Christ is their shepherd-redeemer is by the Spirit's application of these truths to their hearts. They never would come to any of those conclusions on their own. Thus, the relationship of Christ to the sheep is permanent. It is God-given and is sealed by the blood of Christ.

Second, the condition of those who are not the sheep is also described in this particular chapter. The Pharisees who have been asking Christ the pointed questions in this chapter are those who, categorically speaking, are the non-elect. In verses 25 and 26 we read, "Jesus answered them, 'I told you, and you do not believe; the works that I do in My Father's name, these bear witness of Me. But you do not believe because you are not of My sheep.' " So we know that there are sheep, and we know there are non-sheep and we know that only the sheep hear the voice of God and we know that those who are not of God's people do not hear. When the goats of this world hear the preaching of the Gospel of Christ, they have the same reaction Adam and Eve had, following the Fall. They run from the truth. God's Word exposes man's sin and he flees from it.

Third, "What is the relationship between grace and

everlasting life?" God's Word shows us that the gift of eternal life falls upon the sheep. Those whom God has chosen, He has redeemed. Those whom He has redeemed He has sanctified and regenerated by the Holy Spirit. These are the same individuals who are given eternal life. Not one of them lacks it, nor does anyone who is outside of the family of God inherit eternal life. Look at verse 11. It teaches us that the elect of God are redeemed. "I am the good shepherd; the good shepherd lays down His life for the sheep." So we know that the objects of God's sovereign grace are the ones for whom the good shepherd has died. Then, in verse 27, we read that the redeemed are the same ones who follow Christ. Why? Because Christ knows them. That is why they hear His voice and follow Him. Men cannot know God aside from Jesus Christ. The knowledge by Christ of the sheep is not a mere head knowledge, but it is elective and redemptive knowledge. Then verse 28 teaches us that it is the sheep who hear, who follow Christ and who receive eternal life. In summary, then, to this point, the elect of God are redeemed by Christ; the redeemed are regenerated by the Holy Spirit, and those who are regenerated by God are given eternal life. Finally, those who receive eternal life are the ones who hear. Now, someone may ask, "Where did the plan of salvation originate?" The answer to that is "in the heart of God". You cannot pry into the eternal councils of God any farther than that. God has not told us why He chose whom He chose. We know that He is sovereign, and we know that His purposes will be fulfilled. It is not left to chance.

Fourth, how do the sheep hear? Verse 27 says: "My sheep hear My voice, and I know them, and they follow Me." We are not told how they hear, it simply says they do hear. When Jesus says, "My sheep hear My voice, and I know them, and they follow Me," we who believe know what it means. We follow His voice. How could we follow Him if we did not hear His voice? Let me make it clear that it must be Christ's voice that you are hearing. All men answer to some call in life. Some men respond to the call of philosophers. Others to the economists. Others to the historians. But until it is Christ's call that you hear, you are not a member of God's family. You must come to Him and recognize that He is the Good Shepherd and that without Him you are lost. So, I ask the question of you, "What voice is it that you are hearing?" If you claim to be a Christian, but follow another voice than Christ's, your claim is ill-founded. Jesus says seven times in the book of Revelation, "He who has an ear, let him hear what the Spirit says to the church." What do you think Jesus means when He says that? Jesus means that we who are the sheep and know His voice must always listen to His call.

Fifth, eternal life is a gift from God. He has given us this gift of eternal life from which we cannot fall. Yet the question is constantly asked, "Why can't I lose my salvation?" If you can lose your salvation, then it is not God who has saved you. If God is the One who saves, how can *you* be lost? If it is a work of God, then what can you do to undo what God has done? John has given a very strong image here. Picture yourself in the palm of God! There is no way that you can jump or wriggle out of that hand, and there is no way that a man is going to snatch you out of it. (Romans 8:33) What greater security can be offered? There is no security outside of the palm of God's hand. If I am anywhere but in the palm of God's hand I am not safe. I am not safe from myself, I am not safe from sin, I am not safe from time, and I am certainly not safe from the devil who the Scripture says is like a roaring lion, roaming the earth, seeking someone to devour.

The Father's will for Christ was that He die for God's people and that He will not lose one single sheep. Not one! Of the millions of believers across human history whom God has been willing to regenerate, not one of them can be lost. How glorious! Note that verses 27 and 28 say nothing like, "except you backslide, you shall never be snatched out of the Father's hand." If you are not in Christ, you must face Him as a judge and be crushed under God's wrath. It will either be in the palm of God or under His fist for eternity. Which will it be? Do you hear the voice of Christ? Are you still saying, "I can make it on my own?" Are you saying, "It doesn't matter, I'll moralize my way into heaven." You will not moralize your way into heaven, you will moralize your way into hell. What is your response? "All that the Father gives Me shall come to Me; and the one who comes to Me I will certainly not cast out." (John 6:37)